A true story of survival and overcoming

Hand in Hand

Charlene Stoller

ISBN: 978-1-933753-70-6

Text design by: Larisa Yoder
Cover design by: Veritas Creative
Cover Photograph by: Perception Studio
Page 65 bottom photograph by: Drew Shonka Photography
Page 69 top photograph by: Perception Studio

2673 Township Road 421
Sugarcreek, Ohio 44681

Carlisle Press
WALNUT CREEK

800.852.4482

INTRODUCTION

ON THAT FATEFUL JANUARY NIGHT, Scott and I found ourselves very unexpectedly in a hospital room with aching hearts. Could this really be happening to us? Could it really?

I refused to leave him alone—not like this. I found my way down to the hospital gift shop and bought a little brown notebook. "If you tell me what you went through before I got there, I'll write it down." So he did. He talked; I wrote.

Later, I was so glad we had written it down right then because it was still fresh in our minds—a little too fresh. It would become a memoir for the kids—some of whom were yet to be born. This is what happened to Dad.

I started out sleeping on the reclining chair. Trust me, it wasn't a La-Z-Boy. When I just couldn't put up with it anymore, I lay out on the tile floor. At least it was flat and didn't put kinks in my back, legs, and neck.

I'm not kidding; he had the most wonderful nurses you could ask for. Somewhere, somehow, they found me a bed. I hadn't asked for it, and I couldn't believe it! I'm sure it was not standard hospital procedure, but it was the outstretched hand of human compassion. I was very touched.

Friends and family came and went during those next weeks in spite of the raw, bitter temperatures that we had at that time. I asked them to sign our little brown book. Now it doubled as a guest book register.

One by one they began to realize that the account of Scott's accident was scribbled on those pages, and they lost themselves in reading it. Scott didn't want his visitors to come up and bury their noses in the notebook. He has always loved companionship and interaction, and now he needed it more than ever.

Finally, I struck them a deal. "When I get home, I'll type this up and give copies out to anyone who wants it." It worked.

And then came the call from a publisher almost twenty years later. He challenged me to write a book. I was not expecting that. I told him I wouldn't promise him anything, but that I promised to consider it. He told me, "If you'll write the book, you'll have a publisher."

So I stewed about it for a while. I wanted Scott's blessing and God's blessing before committing to anything. Finally, I felt compelled to start, and once I did I couldn't stop. I have suspected for years that I was OCD, but now I'm sure of it. Burning the candle at both ends, I couldn't quit writing.

This project was not exactly an easy one. It might even be classified as downright painful. By its very nature it dug up a lot of events and emotions that were anything but pleasant. I was beginning to feel that I was reaching my limit; I had enough. I wasn't the only one. One morning as Scott and I were editing and wrestling with words, I looked back at him to see the tears spilling over. This was getting to be very tough on him. In order to recall details, he was reliving some very traumatic events. Poignant memories were becoming more and more vivid. He was very supportive of the project, but the more we remembered the more we remembered. Enough was enough. It was time to finish the manuscript and move on with our lives.

My prayer and purpose for this book is to encourage you to build your relationship with the God of all creation (Genesis 1:1), the God of all comfort (II Corinthians 1:3&4), the God who was big enough to grant Scott a complete peace under horrible circumstances. He promises in Jeremiah 29:12-13 that if we search for Him with our whole heart, we will find Him.

Acknowledgments

FIRST ON MY LIST IS SCOTT. Thanks for being my best friend and inviting me to share your life with you. Thanks for persevering for the kids and me when I'm sure it would have been easier to give up and quit. Your tenacity and determination are an inspiration to us many times over.

To our children: Doyle and Naomi, Lynelle and Craig, Nelson and Jessica, Warren and Erika, Toby, Clark, RoseMary, and Melody and our six grandchildren. Thanks for adding a deeper dimension, purpose, and completeness to our lives. We love you!

Thanks to the EMTs, prosthetists, nurses, and doctors (especially Dr. Nicholas Papas, Dr. Yue Mok, and Lloyd Siders, NREMT-P) for your years of study and dedication that make you so valuable to those of us who suddenly find ourselves battered and beat up and our world turned upside-down at times. Where would we be without your skilled hands and your expertise?! Your impact on our lives has been monumental.

Thanks to our parents, Everett and Marge Stoller and Joe and Lilas Rufener, for standing by us through thick and through thin. Believe me, sometimes things got pretty thick!

Thanks to Uncle George Riggenbach, Jr. for asking us to join you on this beautiful farm. You were constant and steady through the chaos during that year following Scott's accident. You had to be.

Thanks also to Marvin Wengerd, who is our publisher and our friend. If you hadn't pushed me out of my comfort zone by encouraging me to put it all down on paper, we probably would never have accomplished this book.

Table of Contents

CHAPTER ONE

Finding Scott

I LEFT THE NEIGHBOR'S HOUSE on January 16, 1997, at around 12:10 and headed for home. I had no idea that while I was in the comfort of warmth and friendship, Scott was in an intense struggle fighting for his very life. The day was bitter and fiercely cold. The wind swirled the snow through the air and hurled it at anything or anyone unfortunate enough to be outside—even Scott.

As I drove in the lane, I wondered whether I should park the van outside until I went to pick up Doyle at school at 3:00 or put it in the garage. I knew Scott was planning to clean out the round baler, so I decided to drive back to the shed and ask his opinion. Normally, I am capable of making decisions. It was a ridiculously simple and unimportant question, but God's hand was in it. It was time to find Scott. I didn't know it then, but God did. Time was running out.

As I drove around by the shed, I found the 150-horsepower Case IH Magnum 7110 tractor hooked to the two-ton New Holland 650 round baler. The back bale discharge door was up, and the machine running. As I pulled up beside the baler, I found Scott. It looked like he was reaching far into the baler with his right hand. It still did not register that anything was wrong. I rolled down my window to talk to him. "Help!" was all he could croak out. Then I got a close look at his face and saw the horror in his eyes. "Shut the tractor off!"

I jumped out of the van with a knot in my stomach, climbed up into the Magnum, and turned the key. The Cummins diesel engine rumbled and shuddered to a stop and fell silent. I clambered down the steps and rushed back to Scott.

CHAPTER TWO

For the Record

AS A YOUNG GIRL, I had pictured living in a farmhouse nestled down a long lane shared with my farmer who was strong and rugged on the outside but tender-hearted and kind on the inside. We had lived on Scott's maternal grandparents' farm for almost a year when the accident happened—just two days short of a year to be exact.

We had previously farmed with Scott's parents and brothers for the first six years of our marriage. At age 26, Scott was given the opportunity to operate his grandparents' farm with his bachelor uncle, George Riggenbach, Jr. We were milking around 80 cows in a stanchion barn and growing the crops to feed them on the 250-acre farm.

Scott and I had attended the same school and the same church. During our elementary school years we were special friends. For my eleventh birthday he gave me a Russell Stover chocolate Easter egg basket and a tiny Rubik's cube on a necklace. He hit the nail on the head with the chocolate, and Rubik's cubes were all the rage back then. I even learned how to solve them; I still like to impress my kids with my puzzle-solving talent. The chocolate is all gone, but I still have the Rubik's cube.

Our fifth and sixth grade home rooms were side by side which was convenient. The drinking fountain was in the hall by his classroom which was also convenient; I hovered by his classroom's open door hoping to catch his eye for a quick smile and a wave.

As time passed, things changed and we both moved on, but we always remained good friends. It wasn't until in our late teens that we realized that God meant for us to spend the rest of our lives together. We got married on March 25, 1990—six days after my nineteenth birthday. My mom thought I would be glad to tell my kids someday that I was nineteen when I got married—since that's much more mature than eighteen.

Don't think for a moment that she held off the wedding because she didn't approve of Scott. In our wedding service we were advised to use our parents' advice as we faced decisions throughout life UNLESS we had a problem with each other. If that were ever the case, then we should find someone more unbiased to confide in. I have been amused many times as I reflected back to those words because it would have never done me any good to complain about Scott to my mom. She would have taken HIS side, not mine! You can count on it! She doesn't even deny it.

My mom also was to become a key player later in our lives as Scott recovered and returned to farm work.

Since Scott grew up on a dairy farm, it was really the only life he knew. He was the youngest of four boys, and bored was not a commonly heard adjective. He learned at an early age that if he even looked bored, his dad would happily remedy the situation.

During his teen years, he and his brothers and cousins would take turns going to help on his grandparents' farm that was just across the road. Never once did he dream that he would some-day own it. They helped Grandpa George, Sr. and Uncle George, Jr. bale and mow square bales and milk cows. They knew how to incorporate laughter and fun into hard work to weave a tapestry of colorful memories. He knew right where Grandma kept the Juicy Fruit gum and where to find the Scot Lad pop stored in the back of the ice bank milk tank.

Rumor has it that one day when some of the boys were helping Uncle George stack square bales in the mow, he asked one of his nephews to get him a can of cold pop. Unbeknown to Un-cle George, that aluminum can was shaken vigorously en route. When he opened the can, the contents exploded high into the air, and there was only about an inch left in the bottom.

As Grandpa aged, glaucoma slowly and steadily stole his sight. One fine summer day, he was baling small square bales while the grandsons unloaded them in the barn. With the tractor in slow gear, Grandpa's simple instructions were to follow the row of raked-up hay with the kicker baler and wagon. Upon return-ing to the field for a load, the boys discovered that the baler had thrown nearly every bale over the back of the wagon and spread them about the field. They surveyed the situation and quickly loaded the scattered bales into their empty wagon. Protecting his dignity, they never did tell him, and he couldn't see well enough to notice.

Grandma, on the other hand, struggled with hearing loss. Somehow, using his ears and her eyes, they managed to get along well. On a different day, Grandma was driving the farm pick-up truck around the field retrieving the bales that missed the wagon after she had baled. The grandsons sitting on the tailgate would jump off and toss the bales onto the back of the truck. Grand-ma always tended to be in a bit of a hurry, and today was no different. She hit a hole in the field hard enough that the row of boys sitting on the tailgate suddenly found themselves lying flat on their backs in the truck bed looking up at the clear blue sky as the tailgate slammed shut beneath their legs. Skidding to an abrupt stop, Grandma hollered back, "Everybody all right back there?" The stunned boys loudly chorused, "Yeah!" Laughing, they hung on tight as the truck tore off through the field leaving long skid marks, since Grandma couldn't hear how fast she revved the engine.

This farm had become home to Scott's grandfather, George, Sr. when he was just two years old. When he grew up and married his childhood sweetheart, they moved a little house here from across the road where he and Minnie set up housekeeping and had their first six children—only four lived. Later four more children were added to the family for a total of eight.

Scott's mother was one of those born in this little summer house. It still stands today. Although it lacks plumbing and many of the conveniences that we consider necessary in the twenty-first century, we sometimes entertain the idea of renovating it for either a starter house, down-sizing, or even a bed and breakfast. The farm homestead is now considered an Ohio Century Farm, which means it has been in the same family for at least a hundred years.

I, on the other hand, really had precious little experience in farming. I grew up in the country with a very large garden, fruit trees, and a comfortable lawn big enough to play ball with my brothers and my cousins. There was a woods behind our house that invited us to explore. There was a jolly creek running through it that we loved to build dams in during the summer. A huge rock was hidden deep in the woods. We dubbed it the Big Rock Candy Mountain, and it was worth the hike to climb and sit on. But it wasn't a farm. I really didn't know much about farming. I didn't know a bean field from an alfalfa field. Let me tell you, my patient husband had to start at the very beginning. He even taught me to drive a stick-shift truck after my big brother had given me up as a hopeless case a few years earlier.

I suppose you could say that Scott had some things to learn as well. For one, he kept track of the gestation of his cattle on a large wheel. Each heifer had a pin with her own number on it. Once she was pregnant, her pin was put in the correct spot on the wheel that would be turned once each day. Then the farmer knew when she was ready to freshen, or have her calf. (That was one of the first terms this new farm wife learned.) However, when I was pregnant with our first baby, I discovered the wheel was sporting a new pin with a darling, dainty, pink heart on it, marking the progress of my pregnancy. The farmer learned very quickly that the farmer's wife did not appreciate being tracked on the heifer wheel. It's amazing how fast that pin came down!

At any rate, when Uncle George asked Scott to consider moving to the farm that we now call home, it was not a simple decision at all. Leaving the farm where he spent a very happy childhood did not come easily to Scott. He had just climbed the silo the day before, scanned the fields that were so familiar to him, and told himself, "If I can't farm here, I don't want to farm at all."

But God has a way of gently guiding us along step by step and rewarding obedience with joy and peace. After almost a year at our new address and a for-real farmhouse of my own, this definitely felt like home. With three children, Doyle (almost 6), Lynelle (4), and Nelson (1½), we were living the American Dream.

CHAPTER THREE

The Accident According to Scott

SCOTT'S THREE-HOUR BATTLE in the baler was fierce, it was bloody, and it was intense. Although he faced the valley of the shadow of death with no one nearby, he found he was not alone. I'll have him tell his experience in his own words:

For we wrestle not against flesh and blood, but against princi-palities, against powers, against the rulers of the darkness of this world, against spiritual wickedness in high places. Wherefore take unto you the whole armour of God, that ye may be able to with-stand in the evil day, and having done all, to stand (Ephesians 6:12-13).

There is so much spiritual warfare going on. I am convinced that this did not just happen. It was orchestrated. I have no doubt that God was not surprised. He knew what that day would hold for me before I went out that morning. He allowed it and provided His strength through it.

When we were growing up, Dad was always careful, and he made sure that we were careful. He told me over and over again, "Don't ever get off the machine when it's running," and I promised him I wouldn't. That day I knew better. I was cleaning out the round baler that I had borrowed from my dad because he was going to trade it in on a new one. A trade-in is always worth more if it is cleaned up. I had used it last.

It was the first year of working on my grandpa's farm. That meant I had traded bigger equipment like a combine and round baler for more outdated equipment like a corn picker and a small square baler. It may have looked to some like a step backwards. I was worried about getting caught in that corn picker because people get injured in those. They lose their arms. I can tell you the spot on the road the day before the accident that I thanked God that I had a safe season. I had made it. The next day I was stuck in the round baler for three horrifying hours.

That morning I was planning to clean out the round baler. The temperature was right at freezing, and I wanted to get that job done because the weather was predicted to get terribly cold that day—temperatures dropping rapidly through the morning. I thought, "If I don't take a nap after breakfast, maybe I can get it done before it gets so cold," which was mistake number one. I should have taken a nap! It would have been safer!

I regularly got up at 3:30 so morning chores would be done before Doyle went to kindergarten. It was important for us to get to eat breakfast together as a family. I was always glad when I could sneak in a nap afterwards. That morning I went out right after breakfast.

How I actually got caught I'll probably never know for sure. There were some hooks on the worn belt lacings. My coat was ragged and shredded. Whatever it was, it was really fast.

I was very familiar with that baler. I wasn't afraid of it. It had well over ten thousand bales on it, and I had baled most of them when I was working with my dad. I had cleaned it out so many times before and never once thought of getting caught in it.

I had the back bale discharge door half open exposing the inner rollers of the machine. There were six wide belts that go around rollers. I had a screwdriver in my hand poking at it trying to loosen the chaff that was lodged there. The driving winds were making short work of the job. With most of the light chaff removed, there remained only a few large cornstalks.

I was standing on the wheel of the left side of the baler and casually reached for a stalk to toss it out. Instantly, my hand was grabbed and pulled part of the way into the rolls. The force of the jerk pulled me off my feet and onto the moving belts. The palm of my hand was caught in a narrow gap very near my wrist. My first thought was, "Boy, this is inconvenient. How am I going to get out?" I did not realize how seriously I was caught. It didn't take but a few seconds to know that I was in and I was in for good.

The continuously moving belts grabbed at anything they could: coats and hood strings. By now the baler had worked me over onto the three belts on the left-hand side. I was caught lying on my back on a moving floor that was pushing me toward the rolls. With a sudden jerk my coats and arm went further into the rolls causing extreme pressure and excruciating pain on my hand and wrist which were being rolled around a four-inch roller. The continuously rolling belts pulled the coats and hood strings tight around my neck. I prayed. The clothing and especially the hood strings were so tight around my neck that I was choking—I simply could not breathe anymore. I removed the glove from my left hand with my teeth, all the while praying and realizing this is what it must be like to die.

By the grace of God, I got my strings untied. Once the strings were loosened, the pull of the baler ripped open the zippers on my two hooded sweatshirts and Carhartt coat. It tore off the flannel shirt underneath my bib overalls leaving rug burns under my left arm. Oddly enough, the coat and shirt sleeves still remained on my left arm, and they were greatly appreciated as I battled the fierce elements. The day registered below zero wind chills.

By now there was enough clothing wedged between the rolls to stop the first three belts I was lying on. The drive roll on the belts continued to turn above my head causing a horrible screeching and smoking. The slip clutch that drove the rollers got hot and caught on fire. I was concerned that the chaff and oil from the chains would also catch fire and burn the whole thing. There wasn't a thing I could do about it. I smelled burning rubber. Then three of the belts burned in two, dropping me roughly to my feet while my right arm was still caught in the continuously turning roller. To this day I can't stand the sound or smell of a burning belt.

This was the first I really had time to think. I took the opportunity to pray to my God and to go over the plan of salvation I was taught faithfully as a child. I was thankful that the preparation for death was made long before now because this was no time to prepare. I had repented, I had confessed my sins, and because of what Jesus did on the cross and the shedding of His sinless blood, I knew I had a promise of eternal life. Unworthy, yes, but saved by grace.

Next, my mind went to Charlene and my children. It was selfish of me to give up and die. I knew then that I must fight to stay alive. By now the turning rollers had created enough friction that my coat began smoking. I was extremely hot on my right arm and extremely cold everywhere else. I realized then that the choice of dying might not be in my hands. I wondered if I would have a closed casket and what it would look like.

With my left hand I grabbed my Sharpie marker from the front pocket of my overalls amidst the shaking and screeching of the continuously rolling, merciless baler and wrote my wife a final note: "I love you Mom. I am at peace." Then I thought of my children. I prayed for each one individually that God would sustain them without a daddy and that one day they would surrender their lives to God so we could be together in heaven someday. I wrote, "I love you Doyle Lynelle Nelson." I put my marker back and remembered the watch in my pocket. I located it and pulled it out. It was 9:45.

Assessing the damage, I could see that my hand was wrapped around the roller in a very unnatural position. At the wrist, my skin was puddled like saggy pantyhose. Looking at my elbow where the clothes and skin were torn off, the muscles looked like the pictures I had seen in an encyclopedia. There was no skin left. I couldn't help but think that my arm looked like a skinned rabbit. The muscles would contract involuntarily when I touched them with my left hand. The touch sensations coming through my elbow were different than anything I had ever felt before.

I started wondering how the doctors would repair me if I did survive. Could they slide that skin back up? I was afraid they wouldn't be able to get it done by chores that night.

On most days the milkman comes between 9:45 and 10:30. The tractor and baler were parked where he would have to move them to turn around to leave. I was confident that within 45 minutes, if I could remain conscious, I would live. I began calling very hoarsely at first, but finally I could scream.

I had asked Uncle George to take the calves to Kidron and get sawdust. Maybe he hadn't left yet and could hear me calling.

Meanwhile, I was trying to think of a way to stop these horrible rollers from continuously feeding me into the machine. I thought of my two pocket knives. If I could cut the three belts behind me, the roller in which I was caught would stop. In reality I knew it was futile, but I was desperate.

I reached into my pocket with my bare hand that was numb from cold. I grabbed my larger pocket knife only to remember I had broken the pin that held the blade in a while before and actually lost the blade yesterday. I tossed it away in disappointment. I reached back into my pocket without much confidence, knowing the other one was so small.

Accidentally, my numb fingers dropped the knife. It landed on the bale discharge pan—three inches out of reach. If I could just get my pliers from the right-hand pocket, I could probably reach it. I could touch the pliers, but my hand was too cold to pull it out. I had put 64 gallons of fuel in the tractor the day before, and I knew it wouldn't run out.

Sometimes the baler would lurch and my vision would narrow, but it never went completely black. I knew without a doubt that if that small focus of sight would go away, I would be done. I had to fight to remain conscious if I was to have any hope of survival.

I actually had a smile on my face; I felt I was almost through with my earthly life. The verse came to my mind from Psalm 23, *Yea, though I walk through the valley of the shadow of death, I will fear no evil; for thou art with me.* Now I understood. Although the pain was incredible, I had no fear of death. Then I thought of my family, and I knew I had to at least try.

A gusty, snowy whirlwind brought back my glove and laid it right at my feet. With my boot I shoved it over to the wheel and worked with it until I had it on top of my boot. I slowly raised my foot to within about three inches of my hand, only to watch another gust of wind blow it away for good.

I was helpless. There was no way I could stop the baler. I was completely out of ideas. I was totally at the mercy of God. I looked at my watch again; it was 10:30. I thought the milkman should be here any minute now. Little did I know that that day—and only that day—the milkman ran his route backwards. Time just passed so slowly. I would scream for help, pray, and look at my watch.

I saw my cousin, Jim, drive past on the road to feed his heifers. I saw him again on his return trip home. He told me later that he saw the baler there and thought something seemed strange, but he didn't want to be nosy. Uncle George stopped in and noticed the baler there before he left for Kidron. He later said that he stared at the machine for probably thirty seconds (from where he was he couldn't see me) and then decided that I was probably okay. A friend of ours was at my dad's and was planning to come up to talk to me about building a grass waterway in one of my fields later that year. When he got to the end of Dad's farm lane, he decided it was too cold and windy and turned the other way. He'd catch up with me another day.

The wind kept blowing my shredded hoods off, and I could feel them brush on the belts behind me. I kept pulling them up. If my hoods would get caught in the rolls also, surely I would suffocate. I wondered who would find me. Charlene was at the neighbors, Uncle George was at Kidron, the milkman was late; maybe a salesman would come. Look at my watch. Scream. Pray.

I noticed my screwdriver lying on the driveway where it had landed when I was first pulled in. Using the pain management techniques I had learned in Lamaze class with my wife, I used the screwdriver as a focal point and practiced concentrating on my breathing. It actually helped.

By now my knees were knocking uncontrollably together against the pipe I was straddling. I tried to clamp my legs to-gether to stop the banging, but I didn't have the strength. Deep purple bruises formed on the inside of my knees. Look at my watch. Scream. Pray.

I tried not to look at my watch at fewer than 10-minute inter-vals. Sometimes only three or four minutes would pass between checks. Time was going slowly. Check my watch. Scream. Pray.

It was 11:00. The milkman had to be coming soon now. Within an hour, Uncle George will be back from Kidron. My face and left hand were bitterly cold. I held them up close to the roller that was hot from friction for warmth. I touched the roller with my hand only to realize I had burned myself. Now I had blisters on my left hand and still felt cold. Check my watch. Scream. Pray.

The roller was continuing to turn, and I could see that it was burning my arm in two. Twice I tried to pull away and leave my arm behind. Each time I pulled, blood would squirt through the rips in my coat and freeze to my clothes, the sides of the baler, and the roller directly in front of my legs.

It was beginning to build up on the rollers, so I chipped it off with my boot so it didn't look so bad. Mentally it was more than I could take to see it get so thick. 11:45. *Surely somebody soon, God. I can't go on much longer!* I had to constantly hold my head forward slightly to keep out of the belts behind me. Check my watch. Scream. Pray.

At 12:15 I saw the most wonderful sight—my wife and two kids, Lynelle and Nelson, pulled up in the van and parked beside me. Help at last! I told her to turn off the tractor, and, finally, the horrible grinding and roaring stopped. "Honey, it's bad. I think my arm is off. Call the ambulance, and call my dad." He'll know what to do. This was just before the days of cell phones. Even my surgeon only had a pager.

CHAPTER FOUR

The Rescue

I **WAS OFF AND RUNNING** toward the barn. The drive was a sheet of ice. I found my way through the milk house and stanchions to the telephone. I dialed the number, still not comprehending that life would never be the same again. "This is 911. Do you have an emergency?" came a calm voice. In a flurry of words I explained our urgent need. They logged my call at 12:16. I called Scott's mom and dad. The answering machine came on. Oh, no! Not now! I left some sort of desperate message and flew back to Scott.

Meanwhile, Lynelle was crying uncontrollably. "What's the baler doing to you, Daddy?" she asked. In spite of his own pain and fear, he was calmly reassuring her when I got back.

The paramedics would know what to do with a person but not an angry mass of uncompromising metal. "Should I call Dave

(Scott's brother) at Sterling Farm Equipment?" I asked him. He agreed and recited the phone number from memory. "And could you get me a blanket or something? I am really cold." I grabbed an old sheet from the van, but it was so thin I knew it was about worthless. I ran towards the barn again as fast as my shaking legs and the slippery sheet of ice beneath my feet would allow.

I called Sterling Farm Equipment. "I need Dave Stoller right away," I told the voice on the other end of the line. "He isn't here," he responded. "He didn't come in today." I was frantic. "I have to have help. Scott is caught in the baler, and he thinks his arm is off." I told him where I was and hung up.

I found out later that Dave was home with his children that morning while Jan went to an appointment. He got the call from Sterling Farm Equipment just as she was coming in the drive.

I flew to the house for a quilt and called my mom to come for the children. My hands and feet were already unbelievably cold. When I returned, Lynelle (4) and Nelson (1½) were still watching from the van and still sobbing. I threw the quilt over Scott and held it there with my body. "Oh, that feels so good! I thought I was going to die. I wrote you a note." My frantic mind was still trying to comprehend. "Oh, Scott!" I cried.

"Should I go direct the squad back here, or should I stay with you?" I asked. He had been alone too long already. "Stay with me," he hoarsely whispered. It seemed only moments before I heard a siren wailing down the road. Those who have never experienced trauma will never know how wonderfully welcome that sound is. To this day, the sound of a siren still goes through me, and I think, "Someone's life is in disarray." Scott is also still affected by the screaming siren and thinks, "Ah! Someone is getting help!"

Not wanting to waste a minute, I raced around the barn and watched them turn down our lane. Waving my arms, I directed them to Scott. Sterling EMS squad, a fire engine, Sterling Farm Equipment (including Dave), Rittman EMS squad, Dad and

Mom Stoller, Mom Rufener, and some neighbors soon arrived on the scene.

Scott was now swarmed with help who in a short time were also frozen in the bitter temperatures. Scott had now been out in the weather for over 2½ hours. I sat in the van and hugged the still sobbing Lynelle and Nelson.

When I saw my mom, I turned the kids over to her. Surveying the situation with pain-filled eyes full of compassion, she quietly said, "Charlene, don't let them keep his hand on if it's only going to be a detriment, un-useful, and possibly even harmful. He would be better off without it if it's like that." My heart within me groaned to the depths of my being. How could we ever make a decision like that? As it turned out, we had no choice in the matter. It was decided for us.

I drove the van away from the scene, parked it in the garage, and ran to the house to change clothes. On my way back out, I realized I had forgotten to change my skirt, but I didn't go back for fear I would miss going with Scott in the squad wherever it would take him.

When I got back to the scene, Rittman's EMS squad now sat where the van had been. Scott still wasn't out, and Lady, the little cocker spaniel, was trying to get near him. They called for Life Flight, but they couldn't fly because the weather conditions were too bad. They decide before they ever answer the phone whether or not they can come.

The technicians were gauging Scott's mental acuity with questions like, "What day is it? How old are you? Do you know your name? Who are your mom and dad? When is your birthday?" He answered all of them accurately until they came to the last one. "Who is the president?" they asked. Not being able to come up with Bill Clinton's name and drawing a momentary blank, he finally answered, "Slick Willie." Those young enough not to remember that era may not appreciate that, but the EMT—a high school friend of Scott's—broke out into laughter and said, "He's going to be all right!"

They had been trying air bags and the Jaws of Life to no avail. The air bags did not have enough force to separate the rolls. The Jaws of Life would start to spread the rolls apart only to slide out, letting the machine slam back down on Scott's arm. Scott's dad had been pleading with them to take no thought for the baler. Dave, with swift action and skill, torched the roller loose and freed his little brother. Scott fell from the baler into a group of waiting arms that carried him to the stretcher where he was immediately covered with warm blankets. The whole time Scott was very calm and kind and kept a presence of mind. He was amazing. Simply amazing.

His first body temperature was 93.7°. The doctor later said that at 89° or 90° the heart can stop. The freezing temperature along with the tourniquet of coats had reduced the bleeding, but if he had been out much longer he might have frozen to death. How many times I thanked God that that part of the awful trauma was over.

Scott had gone out at about 9:30 and after about 10 minutes was caught. He was trapped a little over three hours before they actually got him released. Exactly how he got caught we will probably never know.

I was sitting in the front passenger seat of the emergency vehicle as we started out the lane when I saw that the block garage was smashed. Surprised, I questioned the driver, "What happened to the garage?" Very kindly and maybe even a little condescendingly, he told me that that was indeed how the garage was all along. Inside, I was thinking, "Sir, I'm NOT crazy, and that garage was NOT smashed!" Later, I learned that someone who arrived just before him was hurrying to the scene of the accident and couldn't make the turn because of the ice.

The emergency team had asked me which hospital they should take him to. Jan suggested Wadsworth-Rittman because it was closer to the big city hospitals which was where he was surely going to end up. As we sped down the highway, I glanced over at the speedometer. It was buried at 90 mph. From Scott's perspective, he watched the telephone poles whiz past the window and felt every bump.

The paramedic who was caring for Scott was concerned when Scott couldn't feel where his hand was. During the transport, he had asked Scott what position he thought his hand was in. Scott's answer was not correct.

When we reached the hospital, they directed me to the registration desk and took Scott to Emergency where they cut off his clothes but saved his long johns at his request. He had just started a new pair and couldn't stand to lose them.

I sat in the waiting room until I could go back to him. The ambulance driver came to me and offered me something to drink. He sat down in the chair beside me. I laid my head on his shoulder and sobbed. When he left, the lady next to me said, "They aren't all that nice."

One of the EMS volunteers who was a young, pretty woman with long, dark hair and a sweet smile came to talk to me. When I questioned her about his hand, she gently said, "It will be a miracle if they can save it." I didn't give up hope. I knew that God could handle miracles if it was His will to do so. I called my mom, who was still at our house, to tell her his arm was severely severed right below the shoulder. In the baler it looked like he was in clear up to his shoulder, so there was no doubt in my mind where the damage was.

"We talk of faith when we're up on the mountain
But talk comes easy, when life's at its best
Now it's down in the valley of trials and temptations
That's where your faith is really put to the test
For the God on the mountain, is still God in the valley,
When things go wrong, He'll make them right
And the God of the good times is still God in the bad times
And the God of the day is still God of the night."*

*"God on the Mountain" by Lynda Randle

I went back to the waiting room until they called me in to see Scott. When I walked back, I met the emergency room doctor.

He explained that they had x-rayed Scott's elbow and that it was still good. "What difference would that make," I wondered, "if he loses his arm below the shoulder?" It was then that the doctor explained that although the skin was torn off below the biceps, the upper arm was still good. The crushing, burning injury had taken place between the elbow and wrist. *Oh, thank You, God, for that much more arm!* I think my first thought was that Scott could still hug the kids. My mind's eye could see him at the breakfast table after the Bible story with the kids on his lap squeezing them until they sputtered.

Then I saw Scott, battered, but safe. He might lose his hand, but he still had his arm, and we still had him. He joked with the nurses who had cut his clothes off, "Isn't there something about 'wait till I get your Hanes off you?'" He was kind and pleasant the whole time, despite being racked with pain and fear. We cried together and talked together as I stroked his head and hair—the only part sticking out of all the warm blankets. By then his body temperature had climbed to 97.1˚.

When I went back to the waiting room, Mom and Dad Stoller had just arrived. I shared the good news that the injury was below the elbow, not below the shoulder. They were also thrilled for the extension. Then I called my mom to tell her the same news and that we were headed to St. Thomas. Dr. Nicholas Papas had agreed to take Scott's case, and St. Thomas had an available operating room. Summit Ambulance sent their squad down to pick up Scott. We loaded up and were on our way again.

When Scott asked what time it was, they told him it was about 4:00. "Who will do my chores?" he wondered aloud. "Someone from that big church will be there to do your chores," they assured him. They were right. We were told there were eight people there that night. And for almost a year, someone from that big church was there to do his chores.

When we arrived at St. Thomas, again I registered him while they took him to the emergency room. Mom and Dad Stoller arrived shortly after.

We waited together until they called us back. This was the first he had seen his dad and mom since this horrible episode had begun.

We talked together and cried together. With a smile on his face Scott commented, "This would be a great time for Christ's Second Coming." *Oh, Lord, just any day we might rise to meet You in the air, but until then, keep us faithful and give us wisdom and courage.*

"This will either make me or break me," Scott commented solemnly. How true! *Lord, remind us always to lean on Your everlasting arms, for there we will find strength beyond our own.* Scott was scheduled for surgery at 5:30.

The song that we used to sing as a family gathered around the piano at home when I was growing up came so clearly to me as we waited there:

"Got any rivers you think are uncrossable?
Got any mountains you can't tunnel through?
God specializes in things thought impossible.
He does the things others cannot do." *

My heart was crying out, "I *am* facing the impossible, but I have a God who specializes in that!"

At 5:00 they took Scott to another room to await surgery. The anesthesiologist soon came in. Scott's basic and repetitive request was simple, "Ask people to pray." I kissed his forehead, and then they rolled him away.

*"Got Any Rivers?" by Oscar C. Eliason

CHAPTER FIVE

The Paramedic Remembers

WE MET LLOYD SIDERS very unexpectedly that cold January day. It was an unusual scenario to forge a friendship. He was the paramedic that responded to the emergency call, and he was indispensable to say the very least.

When I asked him twenty years later if he would mind sharing his memories, he told me, "I remember it like it was yesterday. I can still see him standing there trapped in the baler." As his mind took him back over the years, he started getting choked up over the phone.

We decided to sit down that very evening around the kitchen table and visit. As he reminisced, my pen was flying over the notebook page trying to capture his thoughts.

This is Lloyd's story:

A few years earlier, I had started out as a driver for the emergency squad. I wanted to help people. As time went on, the desire burned in me, "If I could only do more!" I decided to take EMT training. I still wasn't satisfied. "If I could only do more! If this is being an EMT, then I want to be a paramedic." So that's what I did.

I was working third shift at the time. I had left work and headed for home. Since I knew I was on call that day, I dressed in my jumpsuit and dropped into bed. Paramedics were sparse back then; I had been practicing for about three or four years. I was averaging 500-600 calls annually, so the chances of interrupted sleep were high.

Sure enough, I got the call that the Sterling Squad needed a paramedic assist for a farm accident. A farm accident? In January? As more information trickled in from Sterling's Squad who was already at the scene, it was becoming apparent that this was actually "more than a farm accident." By now, I was wide awake.

Our crew gathered together: Larry Covey, Trudy Dheel (Arnold), Mike Banks, and me. On the way to the scene, I rode in the front passenger seat helping to watch for vehicles that might not give the right-of-way to the emergency squad.

Sitting beside Larry at a red light, he leaned forward and crossed his arms nervously on the steering wheel. He told me, "I know exactly where we are going. I've delivered pizzas out there." We had more important things to worry about than pizza right then. I was wondering what was in store for us.

I didn't have long to wait before I found out. We left city limits behind us and headed for farm country. We turned down the long lane and drove around behind the machine shed. Our squad pulled up right beside the baler. When our team reached Scott, he was still trapped. As I surveyed the scene, I could see that we were in for a challenge. He was hypothermic. We had to keep him conscious, we had to warm him up, and we had to get him out. We wrapped him in heated blankets.

"*How* did you get inside this thing?" I asked in disbelief.

"I know. You're going to chew me out," Scott responded.

"I'm not going to chew you out," I told him. "You've been through enough already." Then to the medical team I instructed, "Keep this guy talking to us! He's cold!"

I had just been required to take a Farm Extrication course for my medical training. It even included some hands-on experience at Sterling Farm Equipment. It was not an ordinary class, and at the time I did not understand why I was being required to take it.

I also had just taken a special IV class on how to treat hypothermic patients. I chose to take the class at Akron General because they had a reputation for being real sticklers for getting the job done right. I could not have known how urgently I would need this preparation, but God did. He went before us and prepared the way. The information I had learned during those training sessions was extremely valuable to this situation. It very likely was a key component to saving both his elbow and life.

The EMTs were shouting at me to put a tourniquet on his arm. His brachial artery which is the size of an index finger was severed. Our main concern was that he would bleed to death. I refused. I explained that if we put a tourniquet on him, he would lose everything he had left on his right arm. The well-timed classes I had just taken were fresh in my mind, and the information came flooding back to me right then when I so badly needed it.

They persisted. The tension was tight. Voices were rising. The other EMTs still wanted a tourniquet. They disagreed with my decision and wanted to know how I planned to keep him from bleeding to death. I instructed them to use manual compression. I was hoping that the wound had cauterized enough to prevent more blood loss. The fact that he was so cold was probably slowing his bleeding as well.

I called for Life Flight. They refused to come because of the weather. I couldn't believe it. This boy needed help, and he needed help now. Again, I called for Life Flight. Again, they refused. Sizing up the situation, I was desperate, and I tried a third time to convince them to come to pick up Scott, but they wouldn't budge. The driving snow and blustering wind had simply made it impossible to fly.

We had made a circle around him holding on the warm blankets and blocking the wind. Finally, Scott's brother used an acetylene torch to cut the metal roller free, and he was released from the barbaric clutches of the baler. The first thing I thought as we caught him in our arms and I got a good look at his face was, "This guy is not very old."

When the metal roller was lifted, I saw where his arm had been pinned. At the site of the injury, his Carhartt coat was shiny like glass from the friction of the rollers. The coat had acted like a slippery sheet of asbestos. For some reason the coat didn't catch fire, but the friction burned through his arm beneath it. It actually had a deep divot the shape of the roller above it…and it wasn't nearly thick enough for his arm.

We were ready. I had the IV saline solution bags hanging right in front of the heater. Once we got him on the stretcher and in the squad, I immediately started two IVs flowing. Trudy was holding 1000cc bags inside her jumpsuit to heat them up. We needed to warm him up inside and out.

I wrapped a white towel around his arm and asked them to hold it on as tightly as they could. "And if you see *any* red, I need to know it immediately."

I had planned to take him to Wooster Hospital because it was the closest. Scott's sister-in-law, Jan, approached me and asked me to consider heading north to Wadsworth-Rittman Hospital. When I questioned her on it, she explained that it would head him in the right direction to get him to the Akron hospitals. I couldn't argue with that, so we loaded up and headed out. We were riding in a brand-new squad #547 and we were flying. Scott commented that we took that turn on Route 57 pretty fast.

I agreed, "We were up on two wheels!" That kept Scott alert and conscious. Although it was very unusual, at no point during the entire episode did he ever drop below "alert and oriented times three": Who are you? Where are you? What day is it?

Banks was holding Scott's arm. I took his hand and opened it up. "Do you feel that?" I questioned him.

"Feel what?" Scott asked. I silently groaned.

"Are you right-handed or left-handed?" I continued.

"Right," he responded. "It's weird. It feels like my fingers are at the end of my elbow."

"I think you're gonna have to learn to be left-handed." I figured I might as well break it to him now. I was taught to always be truthful with my patients.

That day was traumatic for him. It was just as traumatic for us, knowing that he was never going to use that hand again…and seeing those little guys…

We have kept in touch over the years. I get a family picture each year. I write their names on the back of it and keep them in my favorite book. They are the only family that lives in my Bible.

Chapter Six

The Loss

We went to the surgery waiting room to wait, cry, pray, wait some more, and pray again. *Lord, give the doctors wisdom. Please save his hand. Not my will but Thine be done.*

We called to notify family that he was now in surgery. Before long they arrived to help us wait. The love shown by God's people was so comforting. The television in the background was frustrating when I needed so much to pray. It felt like the devil's scheme to distract our minds from worthwhile things.

Although I hurt so much on the inside, I was surrounded by loved ones, not to mention the multitude of those praying for us, and especially Jesus who had His share of earthly trials Himself.

As we talked in the waiting room, I remember saying, "I really have no idea which way it is going to end up," wondering whether Scott's hand could be saved or not. I knew God could perform this miracle if it was His will.

It was slightly after 7:30 when the comment was made that, since it was taking so long, it was hopeful that the doctor was reattaching Scott's hand. I don't think it was more than a minute or two later when the door opened, and Dr. Papas appeared. The arm between the elbow and wrist was "mash," in his terminology, and the hand couldn't be saved.

His hand was gone. Gone! So that was it. So this was how it was to be. I felt my insides burning as I tried to grasp the meaning. Dr. Papas was very professional. He talked of prosthetics and said that four to five inches of bone was saved below the elbow to which a prosthesis could be attached. *A what? I didn't want a whatever-you-call-it! I wanted his hand!*

The doctor stressed that it was very important to keep infection out. Since the muscle didn't come down as far as the bone, he planned to graft in muscle and skin to cover the protruding bone once they were sure of no infection. Dr. Papas commented that Scott was handling this amazingly well. He was calm and pleasant the whole time. What an outstanding man!

"Better the storm with Christ in the boat than calm waters without Him." -Macduff

But there was no announcement for Scott. No doctor had to come to tell him the outcome. He was living it. As the anesthesia wore off and the fog lifted, all the events of the past twelve hours came crashing down on him. His first thought was, "I still have it. I can feel it." He reached his left hand over to touch his right arm, but it swiped right through. It wasn't there. "Oh, no…oh, NO!" Even in the unfathomable despair of that raw moment of life, Jesus Christ was there—still there—at the side of His child. *He calleth his own sheep by name, and leadeth them. He goeth before them.* (John 10:3&4)

Thoughts tumbled and raged and churned through his mind. He wondered what I would think of him and whether he could still farm. This exchanged intermittently with intense gratitude to God for sparing his life. He could still be there for the kids and for me.

Beloved, think it not strange concerning the fiery trial which is to try you, as though some strange thing happened unto you: But rejoice, inasmuch as ye are partakers of Christ's suffering; that when his glory shall be revealed, ye may be glad also with exceeding joy. Wherefore let them that suffer according to the will of God commit the keeping of their souls to him in well-doing, as unto a faithful Creator (I Peter 4:12&13, 19).

Sometimes I have groaned to God that the fire was way too hot. But He has always reassured me that He is right here beside me and will never leave me.

The nurse from the recovery room came to get his glasses because he had asked for them. That told me that he was conscious, and I wanted desperately to go to him. I knew he needed me. Because they were very busy in the recovery room, they wouldn't let me go. That was so hard because I wanted to be there in those first crucial moments. I didn't want him to have to face this alone.

We went up to Scott's room to meet him when he was brought up. Then they rolled him down the hall to us. They brought me my Scott. I could tell by the look on his face that he was afraid he was done farming. We had just moved to his grandparents' farm one year before, and we truly loved it there. When I asked him about it later, he cried and said, "Now Grandma will think I'm incompetent." But Grandma was so completely wonderful to us and begged us to stay. She reassured us of her desire for us to remain on the farm and told us, "No one in the world could replace you there." She never knew what she meant to us and how privileged we feel to be part of such a fine family heritage.

When it was time to go, I told them I couldn't leave Scott, but I would love to have the kids come to see us every day. I loved those little rascals so much, our Doyle, our Lynelle, and our Nelson. Although I greatly missed them, I knew they had good care with their grandparents. When I was lonely for them, it helped that I could pray for them. It was so good to see them pop their little heads into Scott's room. *Dear God, please bless them, comfort them, and keep them in the hollow of Your hand.*

There was a small calendar on the wall that was shaped like a six-inch square block. It only showed one day at a time in thick, black numbers. It was made to have a page torn off each day. No one had updated it yet, and it still proudly displayed a bold 15. "Oh, if only it could be yesterday!" My whole existence deeply longed for yesterday that day.

We had a roller coaster of emotions, but it seemed that each time I thought of his loss, this was immediately followed with overwhelming gratefulness for what we have left. I couldn't imagine life without him. How would I have explained to our precious children that the daddy they loved so much and who loved them was gone? Yes, I was glad for what we had.

We both came from large extended families, and Scott had a lot of friends and family that came to visit, which he thoroughly enjoyed. To this day, he still remembers the remark one of the cousins made as we contemplated the events that were sorely weighing down on our hearts. He said, "You know, it won't be long and we'll all be laying our armor down." It just helped put it all into perspective. We always need to weigh things in the balance of eternity. Sometimes little nuggets of truth artfully sprinkled over our lives give us the renewed vision and focus that we need. "This world is not my home. I'm just passing through!"*

Someone advised us that it is necessary to grieve a limb loss like a death. I still consider that good advice. Allow yourself the right to grieve so that you can heal and move on. Go ahead and cry…and cry. Then dry your tears and remember all your blessings, and look for the next person you can help out.

People often wondered how Scott could maintain such a positive attitude through it all. He explained that he needed his visitors to be cheerful and upbeat, and if he pulled them down, they couldn't lift him up. It's like the story of the mom who said to

* "This World Is Not My Home" by Albert Edward Brumley

her young son during a busy shopping day, "Did you see the dirty look that clerk gave me?" The boy responded, "The clerk didn't give you that look, Mom. You had it when you went into the store."

Someone loaned Scott some Zig Ziglar tapes that meant so much to him. Zig's contagious optimism delivered in his Southern drawl were very healing. Quotes such as "Your attitude, not your aptitude, will determine your altitude" and "Getting knocked down in life is a given. Getting up and moving forward is a choice" were a huge encouragement.

I remember thinking, "It's so permanent!" Other people might go to the hospital with a broken bone or for heart surgery, but they come out looking the same on the outside. Scott's injury seemed so visible and so permanent. Then one day it hit me like a ton of bricks. It's NOT permanent! It's lifelong, but it's NOT permanent! He'll have two hands in heaven.

Scott and the boys love to sing quartet. I love to listen:
"No matter where my Lord may lead, I'll follow.
I'll bear my cross, whatever it may be;
For trials here will be a fading memory,
When I am His for all eternity.
I've looked beyond this vale of tears and heartaches;
I've caught a glimpse of the land beyond the sky.
A few more days, then home I'll go rejoicing;
I've looked beyond, now the world can't satisfy."*

Scott would sometimes walk the halls at St. Thomas Hospital when he didn't have company himself and stop in to visit with other patients. He heard about all kinds of troubles and became increasingly aware that he was always relieved to come back to Room 815. None of their injuries were as bad, but when he heard about their lives and what they would go home to, he was glad to pick up his own problems.

Then he switched his focus to his visitors and realized that there weren't any of them he wanted to trade places with either.

*"I've Looked Beyond" by Mosie Lister

Sizing it all up he told me, "You know, I just realized something. There isn't a single person in the whole world anywhere that I would trade places with. And if that's the case, then I don't have it too bad."

The spirit of a man will sustain his infirmity; but a wounded spirit who can bear (Proverbs 18:14)?

The nurse consultant, Naomi Carey, who counsels with patients and families marveled at Scott's attitude. Telling this to Scott's mom, she added, "And that didn't just happen." We appreciate faithful parents who taught us how to deal with life and the real meaning of it: to love and serve the Master.

One day, she asked Scott how he was doing. "Fine," came the pat answer. Naomi didn't buy it. "How are you *really* doing?" she persisted. He told her the truth this time. "When we play music, the notes come out in colors and dance around the room. When we play sermons, the words fill up the wall and then come toward me. The sounds of footsteps in the hall or the hum of the heater become warped in my head. People's faces distort when I look at them. Am I demonic?"

Naomi had seen this before. She understood the symptoms. "You aren't demonic. This is a medical problem. You are hallucinating. Some people pay good money to experience what you are experiencing." Away with the Vicodin. Problem solved.

I struggled with how much to help Scott. When they brought him his food tray, the little bowl of salad that was tightly covered in plastic wrap looked like a challenge with only one hand. The cardboard milk carton that we all use two thumbs to open taunted me. The hospital pants he was wearing were complete with a drawstring at the top, and it was necessary to tie them to hold them up. What should I do? If I hovered over him and made him feel helpless, I would crush his spirit of self-worth and value. If I didn't offer to help, would he think I didn't care? It's one of those pop quizzes in life that you aren't ready for. I needed at least a bachelor's degree to properly handle this, but instead I was getting a crash course.

The practice I adapted in the hospital I continued for the next twenty years. I look the other way and know that he will miraculously figure out a way to get done the things he wants to get done. He has a tremendous ability to adapt and cope with whatever comes his way. His capacity to use Plan B or maybe even Plan C or D is an inspiration to many of us who are privileged to share life with him.

I remember someone asking me if I helped him get dressed in the morning. I looked at them in disbelief. I never helped him dress other than once in a while when his fingers would fumble with the tight top button of a dress shirt—especially if he had a crack or a sore on one of his fingers—and the buttons on his left sleeve cuff are not feasible.

Scott still remembers being irritated that when they brought his clothes to go home, they brought his dress shoes that were slip-ons that he wouldn't have to tie rather than tennis shoes. Don't you doubt for a moment that that was done in greatest love and consideration, but the message to Scott was, "Here is something you can't do. You can't tie your shoes." Scott did learn to tie his shoes. He also came up with a special way to lace work shoes that turned out to be faster than most people can put on their shoes with two hands.

During those years there was a young neighbor boy who spent almost every Sunday afternoon and evening with us. Shane was between Scott and Doyle in age. Since Doyle is the oldest of the family and Scott is the youngest in his family, we affectionately refer to him as Doyle's big brother and Scott's little brother.

Shane was a teenager at the time of Scott's accident. When he saw Scott's ingenuity for lacing shoes, he adopted it for himself and introduced it to his high school agriculture class. For a time it became the fashion trend of the Norwayne FFA.

Shane remembers someone commenting at the time of the accident, "I hope he knows how to use a computer because he probably won't be able to keep farming." Realistically, there were probably many people who thought the same thing. "Ironically," Shane continued, "if I hadn't come all those years, I probably wouldn't be farming."

One of the biggest challenges in public was and is a cafeteria-style food line. Usually the tables are so laden with food that there is no ledge to set his plate down to fill it. One time when we were visiting somewhere, he asked a little, old lady who was blind in one eye if she would carry his plate through the line. She was so thrilled to help him. She cried and kissed him as she told him, "I'm so useless!" It made her day to help him. He learned right then and there that he could use his disadvantage to build someone else up by letting them lend a hand. It might be a complete stranger or it might be his own children.

Scott explained, "If I ask a five-year-old to come and hold a wrench on the other end of my bolt, I can make his day. It's at the expense of my pride and ego because with two hands I could easily have done it myself, but if I can overcome that, we'll both be better off. Kids know a difference between busy work and real work. I have the advantage of really needing help at times."

It didn't always work that way though. Once when going through a cafeteria food line at a meeting of farmers, they had hard-dipped ice cream that even big guys with two hands were struggling to scoop. Scott asked the man in front of him if he would mind dipping some ice cream for him too. "I think I'll just let you get your own," came the gruff reply. Then the man turned and realized that he had just spoken those unkind words to a person with only one hand. Scott remembers, "He felt bad, I felt bad, and the ice cream wasn't nearly as good as it would have been."

We knew very few people with limb loss. One of them was a little boy who had lost his hand at age four. I longed to hear from his mother, Pat. I wanted to talk to someone who understood the turmoil in my heart. She sent a message with a friend, "Tell them there is just so much life left." Then a letter came in the mail from her. It read:

Greetings of love to you both. I would love to visit with you in person but feel that your family will be so much more comfort to you at this time. But I want to encourage you. There is a great life after an amputation. Maybe even a better life, if you truly allow the Lord to work in your lives. Scott, I have complete confidence that you will be able to provide for your family. You have a beautiful supportive wife, healthy children, and a faith in God. Your house is in order. You all are going to be fine. There will be many that will look at you with sad, sorrowful, pitiful looks, but remember that they weren't called upon to have this affliction because they could not handle it. Please don't let this type of people pull you down into the depths of despair. My Eric from the first day of his accident had adults feeling sorry for him. But he pays them no mind. He is happy with what he has, and he has found a way to do everything he has wanted to do!

His loss is much greater than yours. If he would have an elbow, the possibilities are unbelievable for prosthetics. Our insurance will only allow us to get an arm that looks like it was invented in the 1600s, and the Cadillac of arms (which Eric would benefit from) costs so much because of the wrist, elbow, and shoulder electronics. But Eric has not wanted an artificial arm yet. He says he doesn't need two arms. He is truly a great kid.

By any means I don't want you to think that I don't ache for you. You will have an adjustment in life, being in your 20s and used to doing tasks a certain way, but you will overcome every obstacle with the help of your supportive wife and children. For our dear God, our heavenly Father, the all-wise One, who controls all things, and whose deepest desire is for your good, has permitted this accident to happen in your life because God knows that you will unconditionally surrender all that you are, and all that you have, all of which belongs to Him anyway. I know you will commit yourself afresh to Him and all the demands of every day, realizing that God has every detail of your life in His control. You should feel honored to be chosen to carry this burden. God will see to it that the burden laid on you is the light end for He will carry the heavy end. No affliction would ever trouble us if we knew God's reason for sending them.

But as life goes on, we realize why certain other people aren't given such a tough load. I have over the last 8½ years been shocked at the immaturity of some children and adults when it comes to life. So many people cannot cope with the simple daily trials of life. They have their arms and legs, good healthy looking bodies, but their minds are messed up. This is by far a worse condition than not having a limb. I would never have understood this if I would not have seen Eric handle life's test. The tests of life are to make, not break us. Trouble may demolish a man's business but build up his character. The blow at the outward man may be the greatest blessing to the inner man. I am having a hard time trying to describe what I am feeling about life and people, but in years to come you too will understand what it is I am trying to say.

If God puts or permits anything hard in our lives, like losing a hand in a farm machine, remember that the real trouble will come only if we rebel what God has permitted to happen. True bitterness will set in and you will live a life of misery and will drag everyone you talk to into the horror of it also. You will meet people like this, as I am sure you already have. I feel so sorry for these poor individuals who complain about such minor things.

I am really rambling on and on and I am sure you are weary from my yacking. My kids also become weary from it. I just hope I can encourage you. When Eric had his accident, I did not know anyone with an amputation personally. I needed to talk to a mom who had been through the same experience as I was going through, so I searched for help. I located many moms who had similar accidents and losses. Do you realize that your parents will probably have a more difficult time dealing with this accident than you will? We hurt so badly for our children. These mothers had experienced the same questions I had and the same pain I felt in my heart, and they said, "It will be okay." Those simple words were so comforting to me because they had been there. Their letters encouraged me and strengthened me and I realized that if Eric wanted to be successful in life, it was possible.

They gave me many helpful hints, but most importantly they all said, "Don't feel sorry for him." So we treat Eric like normal. The older kids give him no slack. He is probably the most organized of all my children. He's got his act together, and I am so proud of him. You have that same spirit, I am told. Most of the greatest people have passed through fire. If you think about it, most of the Epistles were written in a prison. When God is about to make use of a man, He puts him in the fire.

So try to laugh and things won't come so hard. If you laugh at trouble it will not seem so real. I know, for I laugh away mountains and mountains. Jesus told us of the faith that removes mountains. Maybe cheerfulness and laughter in the face of difficulty is evidence of that wonder-working faith. May God give you the faith to move mountains. We will be praying for you and your beautiful family. I hope I have succeeded in encouraging you that there awaits for you a great life after an amputation. All My Love, Pat

Her words were balm to my soul! It was someone calling out encouragement from the end of our dark tunnel. Her "you-can-do-it!" attitude was contagious. How I cherished her letter then and still do today.

One Saturday evening, because a surgery was scheduled for the next morning, he was not allowed anything to eat after 12:00

AM. One of the nurses on the floor snuck in just before midnight and brought him a milkshake that she had scrounged up from somewhere. I'm telling you, they were an amazing staff!

On Sunday, January 19, when Scott went into debridement surgery to remove decaying flesh and infection, the last thing he saw before he went under was the surgery room nurses standing around with tears in their eyes as they told him, "We are praying for you."

During one restless night at St. Thomas we were listening to a borrowed tape when a song came on that seemed as though it was sung just for us:

"There are storms that we all encounter,

Do not fear; they will do you no harm.

In the Lord you will find protection

In the shelter of His arms.

There is peace in the time of trouble;

There is peace in the midst of the storm,

There is peace though the world be raging,

In the shelter of His arms." *

On Wednesday, January 22, Scott was discharged from St. Thomas to go home for a few days before his reconstructive surgery which was scheduled for Saturday, January 25, at Akron General.

It was so good to be home. I felt like we were gathering strength for the next hospital stay.

Scott felt a slight coolness from Lynelle at the hospital which made him feel sad. However, the first night at home before I went to bed, she crept over to him and innocently asked, "Daddy, would it make your arm feel better if I would lie beside you?" Her daddy was thrilled. "It sure would, Peach!" She snuggled up right next to her precious daddy and fell asleep.

Before Scott left the hospital, Dave asked if he should get the baler out of our machine shed so that Scott didn't have to look at it. Scott immediately refused because, "I can't suffer that de-

*"In the Shelter of His Arms" by Ike Davis & Ray E Heady

feat without trying again." He insisted on being the one to drive the baler in to Sterling Farm Equipment. He needed to face the enemy that had stolen away his hand—the sooner the better. He didn't want to wait until hay season.

Word must have gotten out, because there were people waving to him from the front store window as he passed Maibach's Furniture, and the employees at Sterling Farm Equipment were gathered outside in the parking lot smiling and waving their welcome and encouragement. His undefeated attitude and clear decision to "get back in the saddle" were refreshing for all of us.

They had to replace all six belts and various other parts that were either torched in two or burned from friction. We never did receive the bill. It was covered by Sterling Farm Equipment and fellow farmers.

Scott requested that when the time came, he wanted to make the first bale with it after it was repaired. It was all an important part of his mental coping with the aftermath.

A young neighbor boy, Dana, bought that traded-in baler in the spring with the intention to do custom baling. On his way to the field for the very first time, he stopped by and picked up Scott. He still wanted to run that baler. Dana was willing to let him. About halfway through the first bale, the belts got tight and slipped and squealed, sounding just like they did that day in January. Scott quickly turned off the PTO and sat there trembling.

After discharging the partly made bale, he attempted to find the problem. He was still too injured to physically fix it, but he understood that machine very well. He soon discovered that the new replacement belts were threaded incorrectly. It was just a small mistake that was made when putting the baler back together. He could tell Dana how to take the tension off the belts, take the splice apart, reroute the belts, and re-splice them. They were soon back to making hay.

We were told that there was still writing left from Scott's message as long as he owned the baler. Dana's younger brother said he believed God left that there for a reason.

In the time that follows an accident like this, I think it is probably impossible not to get bitten by the "If Only" bug. If only he hadn't reached into the baler. If only I had found him quicker. If only the doctor could have saved his hand. That's why they call them "Accidents." Have you ever heard of an "On-Purpose"?

Sometimes I would wrestle deep within myself not able to accept the facts. "Why couldn't it have been a leg instead, then it wouldn't have been so visible—maybe just a limp? Why couldn't he have been older so he didn't have so many years to carry this? Why couldn't he have been younger so he wouldn't have had the difficult adjustments and the lingering phantom pain? If it had been his left hand instead of his right, it would be easier for him to shake hands with people. For that matter, why did it happen at all? People don't get caught in balers; they get caught in corn pickers." The sooner we accept the facts and stop fighting them, the sooner we heal.

Incidentally, it warms my heart when I see people offer him their *left* hand in a hearty handshake. It also delights me when—without thinking—they offer me a left handshake as well. After all, we're in this thing together!

Chapter Seven

The Reconstruction

When Saturday came, we headed for Akron General for the scheduled 8:00 surgery. It was a long day of waiting, but again there were so many who stood by us to help ease the burden. The doctors planned to take bone from Scott's hip to fuse the end of the two arm bones (ulna and radius) together so they would move simultaneously, muscle from his stomach to cover the bare protruding bone, and skin from his thighs to cover the exposed muscle of his arm that was "degloved" from below his biceps.

When describing the planned procedures to Scott, the topic went to the upcoming bone graft. Struggling for the right words and trying to be gentle, the doctor explained that he would use a mallet-type thing and a pointed piece of steel to remove the bone. Grinning, Scott asked, "Are you talking about a hammer and a chisel?"

Because the bare bone was exposed from below the elbow, in the not-too-distant past the medical team would have been required to remove rather than save it. There was no doubt that Scott was an experiment, and before they decided to take the risk they had to make sure it was a sensible one. There were questions like, "Do you smoke? Have you ever smoked? Do you drink pop or coffee regularly?" The answers were negative. If he had, he would have decreased his chances to save his elbow because the health of his veins would have been compromised. This would have lessened his chances that the surgeon would have even tried.

In transporting the muscle from his stomach to his arm, Dr. Nicholas Papas would be hooking up veins the size of a pencil lead under powerful magnifying lenses with multiple stitches at each vein's splice. Compromised veins did not fit into an equation like that and spell success.

After Dr. Papas attached each vein, he watched to see if the muscle beyond it would pink up to indicate that the splice had worked and the blood was flowing to the extended part. When it didn't, he had to find the kink and remove it. It was not for the faint of heart.

The whole surgery lasted about nine hours, and we were definitely not prepared for the toll it would take on Scott.

As I stood by his bed in ICU feeding him ice chips and listening to the morphine pump whistle, my head suddenly felt strange. "I need to go," I blurted out. Scott's aunt and uncle who were in the room with me took the cue and flanked me on both sides, linking their arms through mine. Starting down the hall my legs felt like rubber. The last thing I saw before everything went black was my big brother, Lyle, rounding the bend. The first thing he saw as he rounded the bend was his little sister collapsing to the floor in a heap. He was just in time to transport me to the couch in the lounge where I presently regained consciousness. The stress of it all finally got the best of me.

Waking up, there were lots of concerned eyes staring down

into mine. They plunked me in a wheelchair and told me they wanted to check my vitals at the nurses' station. I wasn't very happy with it all, but I wasn't in a very good position to put up much of a fight. However, somehow I wound up in the emergency room and found myself in front of the admissions clerk. I guess somewhere during my trip I revived and my spunk returned. I told them in no uncertain terms that I would NOT be admitted to the emergency room. There wasn't much they could do since I was clearly not going to be persuaded otherwise. After a brief trip to the hospital cafeteria, I headed back up to Scott.

While Scott was in ICU there was only supposed to be one person visiting at a time and no one under sixteen. Doyle came up to the hospital with me on Sunday and they compassionately allowed all three of us to be together in his ICU room.

At first his donor sites pained him much more than the actual arm. As those donor sites healed, the pain in his arm became more apparent. I have often thought of that in regard to life's problems. When we have big problems, then the little ones don't seem so bad. When the big problems resolve, then the little problems become big problems in our minds. I am not insinuating in any way that the pain in the amputated arm was insignificant. I am just saying that when they shaved 110 square inches of skin (Scott measured it) from his thighs for a skin graft, chipped a chunk of bone from his hip for a bone graft, and sliced a muscle pack from his stomach for a muscle graft, it was no small thing.

The skin donor sites on his thighs were covered with large pieces of plastic that closely resembled Saran Wrap. They were sealed along the edges because fluid would build up under the plastic where the top layer of skin was shaved off. Nelson innocently pierced the plastic and released the fluid. Everybody got a little excited, but it all turned out okay.

Dr. Papas informed Scott that he would never do another sit-up and that he would never win another beauty contest. He waited a few weeks after he got home before he started in on those sit-ups. With half of his stomach muscles gone, he had a challenge before him. He still likes to say that he has a three-pack now instead of a six-pack. He worked himself up to 50 sit-ups in a row before he was satisfied that he had proven the doctor wrong. Some days I still wonder if Dr. Papas knew what Scott was made of and said that on purpose just to stick a burr under his saddle. As for the beauty contest, I don't really know because he's never entered any.

On Tuesday, January 28, a lady from the infectious disease department came to his room to inform us that a blood culture taken from Scott's arm during surgery revealed a bacteria called Vancomycin Intermediate Resistant Enterococcus (VRE).

They proceeded to place a florescent sticker on the door warning anyone who would enter. A special bottle of soap was placed in the bathroom, and all who came in or went out were to wash their hands. Scott's bedding was isolated and washed with special care in certain chemicals. His paper trash was kept separate and incinerated. When the nurses came in, they wore special masks and aprons. He felt quarantined. We were devastated. Would this horrible bacteria make him lose his elbow or even his life? Would the skin and muscle grafts become infected and decay? Would there be more surgeries and grafts? How much more could Scott take? Had we come this far to lose him now? Where had this monster come from anyway? At that time, the last question was the only one they could answer. They told him he had picked up the bacteria in the surgery room.

"Sometimes God calms the storm, and sometimes He lets the storm rage and calms His child."*

During that night when I was sleeping on the cot beside him, one of the night-shift nurses came in, pulled down her mask, leaned down, and kissed him. "I'm not afraid of you," she said. "You're like my son." She must have been able to tell that we were about to our limit.

This surely must be what the lepers who lived in Jesus' time felt like. Scott believes there is significance to the fact that Jesus actually touched them when He healed them. He could just have

*Unknown

spoken the word. But Jesus knew that those ostracized human beings needed a touch that could heal not only their body but their soul.

Scott's aunt knew of someone from a different state who had this condition. She optimistically offered to call them to find out what the remedy was. She got back to us not a little shaken. "There was nothing the doctors could do. It was the prayers of his people." Why is it that we look to God as our desperate, last-ditch effort when we cannot think of anything else to do? When we are driven upon the rocks, we find the Rock of Ages.

When burdens got so heavy, that I could not face the day,
Then I feel His arms about me, and I hear Him gently say,
"Lean on Me when you have no strength to stand
When you feel you're going under, hold tighter to My hand.
Lean on Me when your heart begins to bleed
When you come to the place that I'm all you have
Then you'll find I'm all you need."*

Scott wanted people to know about the bacteria so they would pray. I told him I didn't think they had ever stopped. Word spread quickly and people went to our God to plead our case. Through it all, Scott's attitude remained, "Not my will but Thy will be done." I asked the nurse what the plan of action was, and her response was, "Wait and see." They had nothing in the hospital that could kill that bacteria. The previous patient who had it was a twelve-year-old girl. She died.

On Tuesday night they came to draw blood for more testing. The next morning around noon a nurse came to inform Scott that, according to the blood test, there was now no trace of VRE. Gone! Just like that. How could it be? Was there a mistake? No. They assured us there was no mistake. Scott did have the infection. They still had a sample of it taken from him that was growing down in the lab. *Thank You, Lord!* The warning sign came down, and we were human again. I don't know if they ever came up with an explanation, but we will thank our God for the miracle and the dedicated people who prayed for us. After that,

*"Lean on Me" by Gary Mathena

Scott seemed to heal quickly and literally felt better from one day to the next.

On Saturday, February 1, Scott had what we hoped would be his final surgery, which was only a small amount of skin grafting. Dr. Papas seemed pleased and mentioned that Scott might be able to go home before long. Incidentally, February 1 was also Doyle's sixth birthday. When he came to the hospital that night, I told him Daddy might come home soon. Choking back tears, Doyle said, "That would be like getting another birthday present."

At not quite two years old, we thought Nelson was too little to understand, but one day he held his right arm and said, "Daddy arm. Baler caught."

Scott had made new clothesline poles for me in the farm shop for Christmas, but they weren't put up yet. A few weeks after he got home from the hospital, he faced the daunting task "single-handed"! Using a manual posthole digger, he somehow dug those holes and cemented the poles in place. I was so amazed. Many times he said that each thing he accomplished gave him courage to attempt the next thing.

Later that summer, he rigged up a stick tied to his right arm with a bucket and helped pick grapes off the vine. He also loved to find a few spare moments and help hoe around the plants and pull the weeds in the garden.

There were many times that I would feel that things were going to be fine. We would be okay, and I had the courage to go on. There were other times when I felt devastated, and I couldn't imagine how we were going to face the future. As my emotions surged from one extreme to another, a new revelation came to me one day: The facts remained the same. It was me that was changing. Whether I chose to look at it from the bright side or the dark side was in my power. I realized that I had some serious choices to make.

Chapter Eight

The Prosthesis

When we left the hospital on February 2, just eight days after his major reconstructive surgery, we thought we were probably done. Little did we know that he had a long way to go.

After giving him the much-needed time to heal, we realized that the grafted skin on the inside of his elbow didn't "fit" right. It wasn't elastic like regular skin and didn't stretch and contract when he opened and bent his elbow. On June 4, Scott had surgery to insert a "balloon" to stretch the normal skin above the elbow. Then once or twice a week the doctor would insert saline solution into the balloon with a needle to stretch or "grow" more normal skin creating the Popeye effect. Scott said it was like a nine-month pregnancy in eight weeks.

Then on August 13, Scott had surgery to remove the balloon and bring the normal, extra skin down past the inside of the elbow. This worked wonderfully and solved that problem. We figured that surely *now* we were done.

Since Scott had gone nine months without his prosthesis, his left arm became incredibly strong from use, and even his shirt sleeves got tight. However, all that use began to show up in his wrist as he developed carpal tunnel syndrome. He got one round of cortisone which worked temporarily but not long-term.

Dr. Papas then offered surgery. He drew marks on Scott's wrist where he would make the incisions and explained that Scott could not use his hand for three weeks afterward. That was more than either Scott or I could handle. A knife to his only wrist would be a last resort, and three weeks without using his hand looked big to us.

Scott started going to a chiropractor and experienced huge success. A monthly maintenance visit has usually been enough to keep his wrist happy. He also has to constantly be aware not to overuse it. Repetitious jobs are especially detrimental. Some of those jobs are best delegated to a boy with two hands.

I have often stared at that strong, beautiful hand and begged God to protect it from harm in any way, shape, or form. Scott copes so well with his loss, but I still plead that his left hand can be spared any trouble.

On October 8, Scott got his first prosthesis with three attachments—two different hooks and a mechanical hand—which he operated from either shoulder. He was so excited to finally have his prosthesis that was to be a big player in his return to independence and end the need for friends and family coming to help with chores each day. I, on the other hand, was staring at this new, intruding bionic arm with a wary eye. This new look would take some getting used to for me.

Ready to share his joy, he announced, "I'm going to show my dad!" I remember the spot in the driveway where I stood when he returned from his brief trip. "What did he say?" I asked. With a confused expression in his puzzled eyes, he told me, "He cried."

I turned quickly away before the tears in my own eyes could betray me. "No kidding!" I thought. I understood why his dad cried. I understood all too well! At the same time, I didn't want to discourage Scott from this new step of progress.

That first evening home with his prosthesis, he chased everyone out of the barn and fought his battle alone as he learned to control and maneuver this new tool to his benefit. This valuable improvement was to become a tremendous help to him in the future of his farming career.

He was scheduled to attend Occupational Therapy twice a week for six weeks to learn how to operate his prosthesis. At the first visit, the therapist was shocked that he came in wearing it. She expected to teach him how to put it on. After watching him operate it, she gave him the ultimate test. He was told to pick up a rolled-up ball of Silly Putty with his prosthetic hook and put it in a cup without smashing the ball or even leaving much imprint. When he succeeded, she told him, "You're done. You don't need me!"

We have adjusted very well to his prosthesis, the kids and I. Most of the time, we don't even notice it. In fact, Scott is so competent with his prosthesis that the boys look on in admiration. There are often times now that it comes in very handy and accomplishes things a hand can't. Scott will jokingly tell the boys, "Just use your hook!" or "You're using too many hands!" Once in a while, the boys will say, "Hey, Dad, can I use your hook?"

His left hand and right hook have learned to cooperate with each other so smoothly and effortlessly that he can go for days without even thinking about it. He does need to be cautious when welding, however. He can easily touch the hot metal with his hook, but when the hook naturally passes it to his hand, it can really create a problem.

One of the boys' friends was watching Scott go about his work on the farm and innocently commented, "Wouldn't it be sweet if you could get a hook to put on over your hand!" Although Scott didn't realize he was being observed so closely, he was sure pleased to have made it look so attractive.

Just a few years ago, Doyle welded a knife blade onto a hook attachment. Until then, the left hand always held the knife and the right hook held the apple or carrot or whatever. Now I don't know how much you know about little boys and pocket knives, but I think almost every little boy who gets a new pocket knife will cut his finger on it within a few hours or at least within a few days. Well, don't you know that for the first time in over fifteen years, Scott cut his finger on a knife.

While Scott made great use of the hook attachment, the mechanical hand rested quietly on the shelf, which suited me just fine. The doctor had told us that even though it had some useful movement, it was mostly cosmetic. He admitted it was more of a mental crutch than a practical tool. I, for one, was not impressed. The hook was a useful, helpful device that made Scott's life easier. I had come to terms with that. The mechanical hand seemed so fake and pretentious. Scott's hand was gone, and I didn't want an imposter.

I kept my opinions to myself, however, because if it was beneficial to Scott's mental coping with his loss, I didn't want to hamper it in any way. He would ask me occasionally if I thought he should wear it. I would always answer neutrally. It didn't matter either way. He should do whichever he wanted. Finally, one day he asked, "Do you have an opinion?" I answered truthfully that I did. "What is it?" he wanted to know. "I don't like it. It's too fake," I admitted to him. The fact is—Scott later confessed—that he didn't like it either but was willing to wear it for my sake. We sent it off to a friend in another state who had a prosthesis and could use it.

The prosthetists at Yankee Bionics have done an outstanding job making very practical, sturdy devices for Scott. They love when he comes in with his beat-up prosthesis because they know it means that it gets heavy use. That's what they like to see. They know that they are making a huge difference in Scott's life.

They make lots of prosthetics for people who will never sum up the courage or ambition to use them.

Scott has two prosthetics: one for dirty work around the farm and one that's clean for when he goes somewhere and doesn't want people to tell by their noses what his occupation is. One year he and the boys went to the Farm Science Review. As he toured the booths, he picked up from some of his conversations that people thought he didn't do anything because of his loss. Finally, it dawned on him that it was because he was wearing his "go-away" prosthesis. Since it looked so clean and unused, people were assuming that he didn't do very much (which couldn't be further from the truth).

In reality, meeting strangers is still one of the hardest things Scott does. He has no reputation built up with them, and human nature wants to make him feel like he has to start at the beginning and prove himself.

Scott was in a store one day when a little boy saw him and excitedly exclaimed, "Hey! Are you Captain Hook?!" Scott was amused and went along with it; he made some quirky response about his eye patch and wooden leg, too.

Scott and his boys do most of the repair and maintenance work on his prosthesis themselves. As of now, Toby Joe is usually the man for the job. Scott has an impressive inventory of pieces and parts. They make a remarkable team-of-two as they "operate" on Scott's mechanical arm on the kitchen table. Finishing up their last project, Toby left the operating room (the kitchen) bragging about being an arm surgeon.

The strange thing is that when he has his prosthesis on but the hook is snapped out to work on it, we gasp and stare and swallow hard because something seems so wrong. His "right hand" is missing. It seems crazy. We don't care whether he wears it or doesn't wear it, but to have it on without the hook snapped in looks so "handicapped."

When the kids were very young, they liked to have Scott pinch their fingers in his prosthetic hook. Three-year-old Nelson squared off and told Scott, "When I grow up and get my prosthesis, I'm gonna pinch you!"

Chapter Nine

Not Done Yet

With Scott back to milking again and most of the greatly appreciated chore help released from their duties here on our farm, we were on our way—or so we thought. He began to notice an increasingly sharp pain at the end of his arm on the top side. When we mentioned it to the doctor, we were knowingly assured that prosthetics just take some getting used to, and most people probably do experience some level of pain and discomfort in the transition period.

Finally, Scott said, "I want to wear this thing as bad as anybody, but if prosthetics hurt this much, people would not wear them!" I am here to say that Scott is neither a wimp nor a whiner, and I knew that if he was expressing this much pain then there must be a reason. Sure enough, when the skin broke through and he started bleeding, the doctor began to sit up and take notice.

On November 10, we met with the surgeon who immediately demanded an x-ray, which revealed that the screw that was inserted during his reconstruction surgery in January stuck out beyond the bone by about a quarter of an inch. The flesh of his arm was being pinched between the screw point and the prosthesis every time he lifted his arm, which tore a hole in his flesh from the inside out. He had to immediately stop wearing the prosthesis to allow the arm to heal. No more milking.

I had been milking in the evenings, but now we were back to the drawing board. Since we did not want to call our chore help back, it seemed right that I would milk both morning and evening until this was resolved.

Scott would get up and do the feeding and all the chores he could. Then he would come back in the house with the kids while I would go out and do the milking, along with Uncle George who also came at milking time. The kids loved having Dad make breakfast, and he learned a few things about being Mr. Mom that he hadn't known before. His specialty was "Frog in a Puddle," which is a piece of toast with the center cut out by a glass and an egg fried in the middle. I think one reason the kids enjoyed it so much had to do with the amount of butter that he was willing to use. Over all, it wasn't a bad setup to get through this pinch.

I feel that God's love language with me is music and song. I couldn't begin to recount all the times He spoke peace or comfort or inspiration to my heart through the splendid gift of music.

A fragment of a song that I couldn't identify came to my heart: "I will be with thee thy troubles to bless." I felt like it was handed to me on a silver platter from the Master. I searched the cobwebs of my memory trying desperately to figure out where that song came from. What was the rest of it? After a few days, it finally came to me; and when it did, I was in awe at the custom-made message He gave me personally. It comes from Isaiah 43.

"How firm a foundation, ye saints of the Lord,
Is laid for your faith in His excellent word!
What more can He say than to you He hath said,
To you, who for refuge to Jesus have fled.

"Fear not, I am with thee, O be not dismayed,
For I am thy God and will still give thee aid;
I'll strengthen thee, help thee, and cause thee to stand,
Upheld by My righteous, omnipotent hand.

"When through the deep waters I call thee to go,
The rivers of sorrow shall not overflow;
For I will be with thee, thy troubles to bless,
And sanctify to thee thy deepest distress.

"When through fiery trials thy pathway shall lie,
My grace, all-sufficient, shall be thy supply;
The flame shall not hurt thee; I only design
Thy dross to consume, and thy gold to refine.

"The soul that on Jesus hath leaned for repose,
I will not, I will not desert to his foes;
That soul, though all hell should endeavor to shake,
I'll never, no never, no never forsake."*

He told me not to fear or be dismayed because *He* was my strength. He told me that the deep waters would not roll over me or be more than I could bear. He told me that He would ultimately bring good out of our deepest distress. He told me that the fiery trial was to refine me. And He told me that He would never, never forsake me. "Praise God from whom all blessings flow!"**

During an office visit, while waiting on the doctor to return after he had been momentarily called out of the room (he seemed to be in high demand), we saw that Scott's charts were lying on

*"How Firm a Foundation" by John Rippon
**"Praise God, from Whom All Blessings Flow" by Thomas Ken

1997. Here we are…six months after Scott's devastating battle with a machine. That strong left hand you see is now the only hand he has. (Doyle 6, Lynelle 4, and Nelson 2 with Charlene and Scott.)

2017, Twenty years later…
L-R: Toby, Craig & Lynelle with Obed, Molly and Ruth, Doyle & Naomi with Lilly and Josiah, Melody, Scott & Charlene, RoseMary, Warren & Erika, Nelson & Jessica with Connor, Clark

Scott grabbed a Sharpie marker from his front overalls pocket and wrote on the side of the baler what he thought would be his final message to his wife before he exited one world and entered another.

Scott wanted his three children to know that their daddy had loved them even if he couldn't be there to watch them grow up.

Scott and Lynelle coping with the trauma.

Scott's brother, Dave, cut the rollers with a torch. When they spread apart, Scott fell into waiting arms.

Scott insisted on facing the machine that took his right hand. "The blood was beginning to build up on the rollers (bottom left), so I chipped it off with my boot so it didn't look so bad."

Scott later demonstrated the accident to show what happened.

This is where he stood when he got jerked into the running baler.

Scott was pulled onto the belts that were constantly feeding him into the baler until they burned in two from friction.

After the belts burned apart, he was dropped roughly onto his feet with his right arm still in the grueling clutch of the running baler. It was in this position that he spent nearly three hours in the merciless machine in raw, bitter temperatures. It was in this position that I found him—still alert and conscious and fighting for his life.

This portrait of Scott was drawn by Melody when she was four years old. It was always amazing to me that our children didn't even seem to notice that their daddy looked any different than any other daddy. I personally credit that to the gracious way Scott carries his loss without complaining and all the poor-me-isms that would easily beset any one of us in that spot. This is one of many pictures drawn of him . . . with two hands . . . two BIG hands!

Children born. Homeschool lessons learned. Meals and stories shared around the old kitchen table. This cherished farmhouse is a shelter from many of life's storms.

We enjoy this beautiful farm that has been in Scott's family for over 100 years. It is an Ohio Century Farm. Our grandchildren are the sixth generation here.

We joined the Organic Valley Cooperative in 2003. It was a decision we have never regretted.

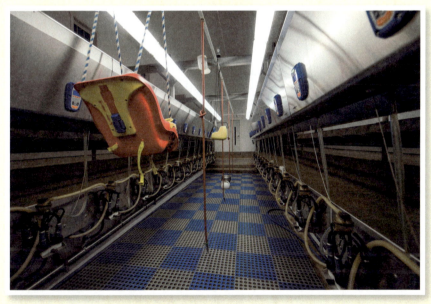

Our parlor built in 2015 is complete with swings for the children to swing in while their moms help with the evening milking.

Scott planting the seed…

…and harrowing the field.

Scott learned to use his prosthesis with incredible skill and ease. He often forgets he looks any different until he sees his own reflection. Warren watches intently.

Here's Scott having fun with his boys (Warren and Toby) in a homemade rickshaw.

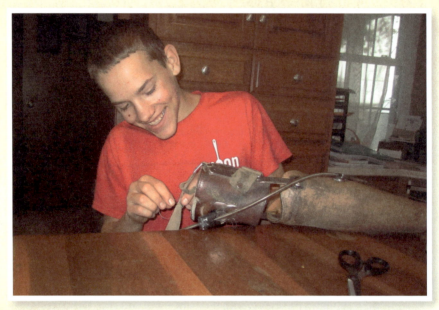

Toby Joe is the "arm surgeon" on duty "operating" on Scott's prosthetic arm. The kitchen table also doubles as an operating table.

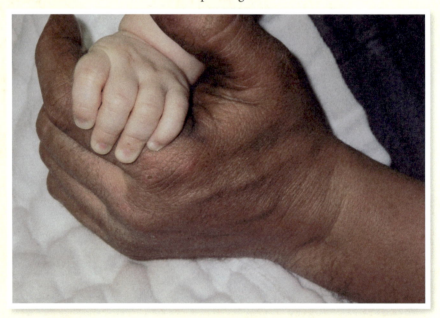

I have often stared at that strong, beautiful left hand and begged God to protect it from harm in any way, shape, or form. I have a special thing about hands now. I suppose you could say I used to take them for granted. I just assumed it was a God-given right or even entitlement. It helps me remember to appreciate the many gifts that He has given us!

As our children are growing up and launching out on their own, they bring us grandchildren to love. As the next generation starts, we continue to trust the future into the hands of our heavenly Father.

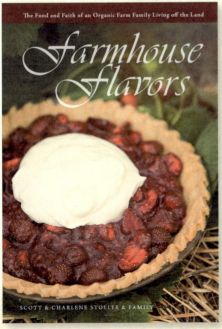

Seventeen years of farm and family letters are compiled in this book along with recipes shared. Complete with pictures from the family album, it follows eight children, dogs, donkeys, goats, and more, living life down a country road on a family farm.

To order call Carlisle Press, 1.800.852.4482

the table. Curiously, we picked them up and leafed through them. Dr. Papas had meticulously documented his work with pictures; and those pictures were both very disturbing and at the same time beneficial. Before Scott left in the ambulance, I had caught a glimpse of his hand. It looked perfectly normal except for what looked like a small bit of hamburger by his thumb. I had no idea that I had looked at his right hand for the last time. I confess that I did have some nagging doubts when I was told it couldn't be saved. It had looked so healthy.

However, when I saw the gut-wrenching picture of the actual injury where the roller had burned by friction more than halfway through the bone of his forearm and read the account written by the doctor including the presence of gangrene, I finally understood.

There were many people who offered to help in any way they could. I remember someone saying, "I know I can pray, but I want to do more!" Scott organized a few work days for those who wanted to participate. He spent hours and hours preparing for them, doing what he could do so they could do what he could not. He made sure he had enough and the right materials on hand and the projects well thought out. It made it fun for everyone because they were able to get a lot accomplished.

The farmers weren't the only ones who reached out to us. We received over 600 cards as well as monetary gifts—some from people we didn't even know. Food filled our freezers. I had some dental work done shortly thereafter; when I got to the front desk to pay, I was told that there was no charge. *Cast thy bread upon the waters; for thou shalt find it after many days* (Ecclesiastes 11:1). I trust the Lord has been their rewarder.

On December 2, Scott had a surgery to remove the too-long screw. This surgery that was simply to back the screw out of the bones was expected to be fairly minor, so he only had to be given a local anesthetic. That meant he was still conscious during the procedure. Since it had been almost a year, the bones had fused together enough, and nothing more was necessary but to remove the offending screw.

Scott definitely has a tendency to overreact to medicines, and this was no exception. I was standing beside his bed as he was in the surgery waiting room before being wheeled back to surgery. Suddenly he quietly said, "I'm going. I'm going." Although that seemed like a strange thing to say, as I watched his face he seemed to be peacefully sleeping. After a few minutes he took a shuddered breath and opened his eyes wide. I never forgot the words he told me. He said, "I felt like I was flying. I was out of here. It seemed as if I would have looked back over my shoulder, I would have seen earth behind me. When I thought of myself, it got dark. When I thought of Christ, it got light. When that day comes, we don't want any extra baggage."

Not really knowing to this day why that happened, I can only surmise that he had what I call (for the lack of a better term) a death trip or an "out-of-body experience" as a reaction to the medicine given him. Either way the message is clear that our hope of eternal life is in Christ…in Christ alone. All that we have ever done or could ever do is insufficient.

"In Christ alone my hope is found
He is my light, my strength, my song
This Cornerstone, this solid ground
Firm through the fiercest drought and storm
What heights of love, what depths of peace
When fears are stilled, when strivings cease
My Comforter, my All in All
Here in the love of Christ I stand."*

One major, unforeseen problem that resulted from this surgery was the fact that his anesthetic was a local instead of a general anesthesia. This means that he was awake and alert—but for the first time in almost a year, there was no pain in his arm. NO PAIN! As the medicine wore off and the load of pain returned, he almost went crazy. The pain that had originated at the time of the accident was excruciating. It slowly lessened over the months, but it was still very much there. Scott has an un-

*"In Christ Alone" by Stuart Townend and Keith Getty

believable ability to manage pain, but when he experienced the complete relief for about 12 hours that day, it was almost more than he could handle when it returned.

The doctor recommended five to six weeks of rest for his complete recovery, so we were back to business as usual. Or not. I was becoming increasingly exhausted with the regime I was following. Scott's cousin, Denise Baltic, was still helping out through the end of the year, and she was so wonderful to have around. They actually were born just days apart, and their moms (sisters) were in the hospital at the same time.

Denise had just graduated from veterinary school and had not taken a job yet. She was good at taking care of the cows, good at milking, good with us adults, and good with a certain little six-year-old boy who still twenty years later speaks with great fondness of her when her name comes up.

But I was still so tired that I could hardly go on…so tired that on New Year's Day, my body simply didn't get up to do the morning milking even though I had every intention to. Although his five to six weeks weren't up, Scott decided it was his cue to try milking again. It worked well, and he was good to go.

It wasn't long afterward that we came to understand that my exhaustion wasn't all caused by the milking schedule. It had a lot to do with our fourth baby—a sweet, little boy—who was tucked safely inside until September. Warren Everett joined the family as our first child born after the trauma.

When he first arrived, Scott marveled with inexpressible joy that this little boy actually had two hands. Common sense tells us that of course he knew better than to doubt that—but when we are pushed to the extreme, common sense doesn't always rule.

Warren was about seven years old when he abruptly asked in an astonished voice, "Dad, what happened to your hand?!" He hadn't noticed before. Although it seems almost unbelievable, I personally credit it to the gracious way Scott carries his loss without self-pity and complaining.

CHAPTER TEN

The Thing Called Phantom Pain

POSSIBLY ONE OF THE HARDEST and perhaps most misunderstood things about a limb loss is phantom pain. What isn't there hurts. Years ago, doctors believed that this phenomenon was simply a figment of the imagination. Scott's surgeon assured us that this is not the case. He explained that even though Scott's hand was not there, the nerves that went to the hand are still there and they have been traumatized. He likened it to sciatic pain that actually begins in the back. The discs in the spine have been herniated or damaged, which pinches the nerves that extend to the leg. The problem is in the back, but the leg is what hurts. "It's the same with phantom pain," Dr. Papas told us. "The nerves are still there even if the hand is not. This pain is not your imagination."

At that time, we used hydrogen peroxide at 50% strength

to prewash the milk pipelines in the barn. If you accidentally splashed it on you, you knew it! It stung and tingled and burned and temporarily turned your skin white. Scott said that was the best way he knew to describe how the phantom pain feels. Also, for many years following the accident, he would randomly get shocked in his arm. It felt every bit like touching an electric fence.

Our babies and toddlers used cloth diapers as security blankets, so there were usually plenty lying around. When he would sit down at the table he almost always tucked a diaper under his right elbow to rest it on. Even the vibrations coming from people walking on the floor were enough to really increase the pain. When he drove the tractors, he would simply hold it in the air rather than lay it on the armrest.

Dr. Papas stiffly warned him to abstain from any significant intake of alcohol because of his phantom pain. He explained that he would be highly susceptible to becoming addicted because the alcohol would temporarily mask and/or dull his pain. Once Scott experienced that relief, he would fiercely crave it.

Scott actually received a couple of letters from inmates he didn't even know who had read his story in *Guideposts*. They were amputees who fell slave to alcohol to cover their phantom pain, and they were warning Scott against it. One inmate wrote to him, "After my third DWI, I lost most of what was left of my life."

When we told one of his doctors about his phantom pain, we were told, "There is no excuse for pain. We can fix that." That was wonderful news, and we plunged right into the program. They gave him Paxil, which is an antidepressant, and Dilantin, which is an anticonvulsant medicine. Scott was not depressed nor was he having convulsions, but we were told that this combination would take phantom pain.

It did. It took his phantom pain. It took his taste. It took his emotions. It took his memory. It took his ability to reason. It took his whole personality. Throughout the aftermath of the accident until then, we had walked together, cried together, and talked together. Now I walked alone…and I cried alone.

When I tried to talk or reason with him, he would zone out. He was a zombie. I told him, "I can deal with losing your hand; I cannot deal with losing you." On the flip side, this medicine did take his pain, so should I, as his wife, tell him not to take it? I remember stepping out onto the porch and weeping.

"God sees the tears of a broken-hearted soul,
He sees those tears and hears them when they fall,
God weeps along with man and takes him by the hand,
Tears are a language God understands.
When grief has left you low, it causes tears to flow,
Things have not turned out the way that you had planned,
But God won't forget you; His promises are true,
Tears are a language God understands."*

I have often wondered why we have to experience so much hurt and heartache in order to grow spiritually. I have even thought that maybe if I would try very hard to listen closely and learn quickly, maybe I could avoid some of life's painful experiences. It somehow doesn't seem to work that way though. Christ definitely didn't exempt Himself from human suffering, and most assuredly "the disciple is not above his Master" (Matthew 10:24).

One day Scott told me to hide his medicine. I didn't understand. "Why? I can't hide your medicine," I told him. Later he said the reason was because he wanted to take the whole bottle at once. "You can't do that! It's suicide!" The effects of the medicines on Scott were terrifying and devastating. I never felt physically threatened, but he was a different person; and through his mental, drug-induced fog, he simply could not connect dots.

He didn't care about anything. He even told me, "Someone could stab me in the back, and I wouldn't care." Something was definitely not right, and this was definitely not my Scott. Scott, who was typically so patient, kind, calm, and rational, was short-

*"Tears are a Language" by Gordon Jenson

fused and irrational.

For example, there was a retaining wall at church that I think about every kid who ever attended there (including both Scott and me when we were growing up) walked back and forth on. On this particular evening, he was so exasperated at the kids for walking on the wall after church. I was shocked. I have always believed that parents should present a united front for their kids and any parenting disagreements should be behind closed doors. I couldn't side with the kids, but I couldn't blame them either. I was trapped.

I called the doctor who had prescribed these remedies and told him, "This is too much medicine for this man." I was calmly assured that he just needed more time to adjust. He predicted it would eventually level out. I insisted, "You don't understand! This is too much medicine for this man." I got nowhere. I hung up the phone.

Miraculously, Scott decided to wean himself off of his medicine. I couldn't believe it, but he did it. One morning at breakfast, I served fresh peaches and pancakes. He commented about how wonderful the peaches tasted. I was puzzled. They were just peaches. Next he was simply amazed at how delicious the pancakes were. Now I was really puzzled. Pancakes were not typically even his favorite breakfast food. Then the revelation came to us. The medicine had dulled his taste buds, and he was tasting for the first time in weeks. Everything was so fantastically good!

To this day, I truly consider it the divine intervention of God's Holy Spirit that Scott had the presence of mind to make the decision to stop taking that medicine. I eventually asked him why he did it. He didn't really know why other than he said it seemed like I cried a lot. He doesn't even remember much at all about that span of time. It was just a fog. The one thing he does remember is that, "Everybody seemed so unreasonable!"

No medicine meant that he was back to carrying the phantom pain—twenty-four/seven. Good-bye, medicine. Hello, pain.

II Corinthians 4:16-17 spoke to me loud and clear: *For which cause we faint not; but though our outward man perish, yet the inward man is renewed day by day. For our light affliction, which is but for a moment, worketh for us a far more exceeding and eternal weight of glory.* He said our afflictions are light and brief, and it will be worth it all when we get to heaven.

Scott manages his phantom pain with exceptional mental strength and resolve. He honestly could predict the weather better than the meteorologists. He would say, "My arm says it's going to rain," or "I don't know if we'll get any rain or not, but we'll see it and smell it." There are still times that other farmers will consult with Scott to get his opinion about the weather before they make a decision about whether to mow hay or work ground. To this day, if his weather prediction based on the level of pain in his arm does not agree with the meteorologists' weather prediction, he will usually go with what his arm is telling him.

One technique he discovered was to mentally designate a day to deal with the many frustrations that are a result of his limb loss. This stemmed from a conversation that he and a friend had about worry. He told Scott, "If you are going to worry about something, then set aside a day and do it right; but only worry on that day."

That stuck with Scott and he decided to set aside a day—which is the anniversary of the accident—to deal with the pain and frustrations of his loss. So if during the rest of the year it wants to bother him, he reminds himself, "This isn't the day. It's a rough deal, and it's worth some time, but not today." It is very effective for him, but it does often make January 16 one tough day. We get together each year with two other families, marking the anniversary of the accident. Scott appreciates their friendship and support very much.

Henry Nouwen once wrote, "Where there is a reason for gratitude, there can always be found a reason for bitterness. It is here that we're faced with the decision. We can decide to be grateful or to be bitter."

We usually make a large circle holding hands around the table to pray at mealtimes. Toby happened to be seated at Scott's right, and normally he would either hold his arm or his hook if he happened to be wearing his prosthesis. That day Scott was not wearing his prosthesis, and Toby pretended to grab his dad's hand beyond his stump where it would have been. Scott, who had been looking the other way, jumped in surprise and turned toward Toby, "What did you do? I felt that!" He literally felt Toby grasp his hand that wasn't there. I cannot explain it, but I know it happened. We are "fearfully and wonderfully made" (Psalm 139:14).

One morning, Scott had read the Bible story after breakfast about Jesus healing the sick and lame and diseased. The crowds followed Him wherever He went and brought Him their loved ones to be made whole. Why wouldn't they?! We were explaining this to the kids and trying to make it real. I said, "That would be like if Jesus was healing people in Wooster right now. We'd be there!" Scott couldn't think of any specific needs and asked puzzled, "What for?" I looked at him in disbelief. He had actually, temporarily forgotten his own loss.

Scott could and still does feel his hand and fingers. He can move them in his mind just like he did normally. If he's distracted sometimes he might walk right into a door because he thought his hand had grabbed the knob and turned it first. If someone tossed him a ball, it would drop right through where his hand should have caught it.

He still has phantom pain pretty much all of the time. Some days he has less, and some days he has more. This is usually based on the weather. He has learned to cope with it because he has trained his mind not to focus on it.

"We pray for blessings;
We pray for peace,
Comfort for family, protection while we sleep.
We pray for healing, for prosperity.
We pray for Your mighty hand to ease our suffering.
All the while, You hear each spoken need;
Yet love is way too much to give us lesser things.

'Cause what if Your blessings come through raindrops?
What if Your healing comes through tears?
What if a thousand sleepless nights are what it takes to know
     You're near?
What if trials of this life are Your mercies in disguise?

What if my greatest disappointments
Or the aching of this life
Is the revealing of a greater thirst this world can't satisfy?
What if trials of this life
The rain, the storms, the hardest nights
Are Your mercies in disguise?"*

*"Blessings" by Laura Story

Chapter Eleven

Recovering

When it comes to recovering from something extremely traumatic and devastating, there's no substitute for time. God's ways are not our ways, and time to Him is not counted the way we count time (Isaiah 55:8-9).

Scott spent many hours in the month that followed his amputation resting on the couch with his arm propped up on a pillow. Even the vibrations that ripple through an old farmhouse that is the home of active kids caused him pain.

Before the accident happened, he had borrowed his mom's accordion and was just starting to learn to play it. Instead of wallowing in self-pity because that was no longer a possibility, he moved on to the next thing, which happened to be a harmonica. Redeeming the time, Scott learned to play that harmonica, and he learned to play it well. "When life gives you lemons, make lemonade," was some of his favorite advice.

Often Scott would start playing at bedtime while I was getting the kids ready for bed. Many were the nights that the children heard the sweet, happy lilt of the harmonica wafting through their heads as they drifted off to sleep. In fact, Warren told me that he considers it among his fondest childhood memories.

Just four months after Scott lost his hand, his grandpa died and the family sold us the first half of the 250-acre farm. Sometimes I marveled at their confidence in us. Scott wasn't even able to do his own milking yet. Seven months after that, his grandma also died and they sold us the second half of the farm. The family members were all *so* good to us, but when you total the price of the farm in addition to the cost of the cows and the feed, the bill was staggering to these two kids.

Between buying the farm, Scott's loss, a new baby, etc., sometimes the combination of everything threatened to be overwhelming. I found comfort in *For God hath not given us the spirit of fear; but of power, and of love, and of a sound mind* (II Timothy 1:7). He reminded me not to be afraid but to find stability in His strengths: power, love, and a sound mind.

On our first Sunday back to church after many weeks, the sunshine was brilliant and exhilarating after the severe winter temperatures that we had been having. The sunbeams streaming in the windows after the cold, hard winter were an allegory of the joy and optimism returning to our lives after the difficult, trying times. It seemed so very fitting. Someone chose the song:

"Yet the Lord is ever near us;

He does guide our vessel's course;

He would test our love and firmness,

Giving storm and wind their course."*

During the spring following Scott's accident, another local farmer lost his life in a farming accident. He was the father of a large family. Scott said that he could literally feel the prayers shift as sympathy for this family's tragedy took people's attention—as

*"Ship of Faith" Author unknown

well they should have.

Nevertheless, Scott temporarily dipped, and he told me, "You would have been better off if I would have died in the baler." I leveled with him right then and there and told him just what I thought of that. I said I would listen to all manner of grief and struggles and heartaches, but I would *NOT* listen to that. That was the first, last, and only time he ever told me any such thing. In confiding to a friend, she concluded, "He was testing you." I'm not sure I'm always prepared for the exam.

At first Scott had nightmares and flashbacks from his trauma in the baler. Just months after the accident, two-year-old Nelson was playing with a 1/16 toy New Holland round baler. He had the back door up and was reaching his hand inside. Scott stepped into the room and saw his son in that position. He shook from head to toe and collapsed into a chair, not even able to identify the cause. When he finally regained his voice, he whispered, "Please, Son, don't reach in the baler."

One night while lying in bed, he felt an annoying hangnail on his finger. It was keeping him awake, so he got up to trim it. It was on the way to the bathroom to get a clippers that he realized it was on the wrong hand. The feeling in the right hand was still so real that it was hard to decipher between what was actual and what wasn't.

Many years later, one morning I awoke to Scott shaking with sobs beside me. He brokenly explained that he had just had a very vivid dream that the whole episode years ago was a dream and he still had both hands—only to wake up to reality and know that won't happen until heaven.

Scott has learned to use all the fingers on his hand in ways that most of us don't even know how. Dr. Papas had told him that most of us don't even use our last two fingers, "They are just along for the ride." Scott says if he were to get his right hand back now, he'd be a monkey.

He also uses his teeth and even sometimes his toes. Once

when the boys were still very young, he was fixing his traveling feeder by himself; he took off a shoe and sock and held a punch with his toes. He has found, however, that it is now much easier to use the boys. Scott likes to say that he isn't handicapped until he loses his teeth.

It is actually pretty often now that someone will remark to Scott, "I sure thought of you this week!" Without even being informed of the rest of the details, Scott will knowingly respond, "What did you do to your hand?"

It is very predictable that they somehow injured their hand and are temporarily only using one. When they are put in that situation, they almost always think of Scott.

Bureau of Workers Compensation (BWC) was involved because he was employed by his grandparents at the time. Let me tell you, they were so good to us. They worked alongside us and helped in any way they could to get him back to work long-term.

One disagreement came up early on when they forbade him to get back to work because he still had a lot of healing to do. He wasn't allowed to do anything, or they would stop paying for his chore replacements. Scott pleaded with them to allow him to do the little jobs he could. He explained that it would help him recover quicker that way. In the early days, sometimes all he could do was push a broom and sweep the feed in the alley to the cows. That soon led to getting the hay down from the barn floor above, and little by little he would take the next steps. It also helped him stay up-to-date with the cows and their lactations. They finally saw it his way and allowed him to do that.

Doyle was in kindergarten at Heritage Private School at the time of the accident. He liked his teachers and he liked the other students, but he became increasingly dissatisfied with going to school. With both concern and determination, he told his dad, "If I would have been home, I could have gone for help!" Talk about six going on sixteen. He started to develop stomachaches at school time, and we weren't sure what to do with him. Finally,

I told him, "Doyle, we are not quitters. You have to finish this year of school. Then we'll decide about next year." That sufficed for the time being. He squared his shoulders and finished up the year; and that was the last of going to school for him. We started homeschooling the next year.

True to his word, he would often get up around 5 a.m. to get his school work done. He never appreciated school interfering with a man's work. He literally became Scott's right-hand man at a very young age. Scott credits homeschooling as a major component to the success of this farm because the kids had more time and interest to learn and work right beside us when their lessons were done.

Warren (1998), Toby Joe (2000), Clark (2003), RoseMary (2005), and Melody (2008) were all born after the injury. They never knew him any other way. Periodically they would draw pictures of Daddy and Mommy, and they almost always drew him with two hands. They simply didn't see him as any different.

When they were looking through pictures one day, there was one of Scott before the accident with two hands. Nelson asked RoseMary who was about five at the time, "Do you notice anything different about Dad?" RoseMary studied the picture and stated, "He doesn't have glasses." He wore contacts before he lost his hand.

Scott has a significant, vertical scar on his abdomen from where the surgeon took his stomach muscle to wrap around the protruding arm bones. Years later Doyle ran into a barbed wire fence that tore a gash in his stomach. Warren observed, "Look! Doyle is growing a scar like Dad's!"

Many, many times we have laughed to lighten the load. *A merry heart doeth good like medicine* (Proverbs 17:22). One morning when we still milked in the stanchion barn, a cow delivered a swift, sideways kick to Scott's knee. Scott declared that he was just fine, but as he would walk along, his knee would buckle and give out on him. He was still determined to keep going. Surveying his dad's circumstances and imitating his persistent spirit, Nelson draped himself over a gate and declared, "I'm fine! I've still got one good arm and one good leg. I'll be okay." It was later determined that Scott had a torn MCL that healed nicely with a borrowed brace and a stationary bicycle to strengthen his upper leg and knee.

Five of the children never saw Scott with two hands. As babies, they would chew on his prosthesis, tug on the cable, or grasp the hook. They would reach up to him with one hand to be picked up instead of the usual two.

I remember watching one of the boys when he was washing his hands. He was holding them under the water and rubbing his fingers up and down the palm of that same hand. I was frustrated and explained, "Just rub your hands together!" Eventually I realized that he was washing his hands like his dad does. I smiled and never brought it up to him again. After all, he did get his hands clean. As an adult, Nelson says, "It's just unnatural to rub your hands together to wash them."

Scott's uncle asked him how he got his hand clean. Scott answered, "I wash my hair." Thinking Scott misunderstood the question, he asked him again, "How do you wash your *hand*?" Again, Scott answered, "I wash my hair!" Finally, he got it! Then Scott added, "Let's hope I never go bald!"

One evening as we sat around the table, the conversation turned to being right-handed or left-handed. Scott verbally counted himself on the left-handed side. My brother, Lyle, expressed his surprise, "I didn't know you were left-handed!" Then he groaned as he realized what he had just said, but Scott took it as a compliment. That meant it wasn't conspicuous to those around him.

My mom helped Scott a lot on the farm during those first years when the children were still small. I always said no job was too big, or too small, or too dirty for her to get involved. She plugged away right beside him and enjoyed it.

She loved working on the farm with her dad when she was growing up, and she continued after she was married until he passed away and they sold the farm. This was like old times for her. She made a big impact on Scott as he coped with the many adjustments of those early years. She was patient and sympathetic when he needed it, but she didn't cut him any slack when he didn't. She pushed him along. Some might call it tough love.

In those days, when the boys were younger, we were sometimes short of man power. My dad and my brother, Lyle, were at our beck and call when we needed someone to work ground, haul silage, or unload bales. My dad used to tell people that he was going to retire to the farm.

I did notice, however, that they all took great pains to avoid learning how to milk. They knew better. There was an end in sight to field work, but if they learned how to do the daily chores, they might get more than they bargained for.

Uncle George stayed on and helped out with milking and various jobs until he retired. He always made time for any projects the kids dreamed up. He would actually take milkers off the cows and let them sit in order to fix a tricycle seat or mix up barn lime for Nelson and Lynelle to make mud pies. We are indebted to him for convincing us to join him in farming the Riggenbach homestead.

Uncle George gave two-year-old RoseMary a bag of mixed chocolate candy for her birthday, which of course we all shared. Clark told Uncle George later, "Rosie liked her candy, but she wishes there was more."

There were a lot of people who pitied us and sympathized with us, but there was one lady who gave me no sympathy. None. She had lost her young husband very unexpectedly, and she had four little children who she raised alone. By this time her children were grown, and she was a grandma. Her quiet words to me were, "But you still have him." After all these years I still remember that, and I truly loved her all the more for it.

Chapter Twelve

The Transition

Scott was raised on a conventional dairy farm. He loved the farm life, and he loved working alongside of his dad. He loved the smell of planting corn in the spring. The words "planting time" energizes farm kids across the nation as they envision the upcoming season with undaunted optimism. "Surely this is the year for the bumper crop." He remembers his dad warning him not to breathe the dust or touch the coated seed or swirl his fingers through the insecticide when they were filling the planter. That puzzled him. He wondered why they would put it on the feed for the cows if it was so bad for him. Perhaps that was when the "seed" was planted in his mind.

Later as a teenager in high school, Scott's open-minded ag teacher invited various types of farmers to speak to the class. One of them was an organic farmer. Until then, Scott's impression of organic farming included lots of weeds because the farmer had revolted against what was being taught as progressive. We later coined the term: organic by neglect. This meant that the farmer didn't put chemicals on his crops, but he didn't manage the weeds or fertility of his soil either.

In the ag classroom, the organic farmer presented it in a much different light and explained things like working with the soil, crop rotation, and alternative methods of weed control. The "seed" that was planted in his mind many years ago sprouted and took root, but when it came right down to it, he was still convinced that it couldn't be done.

Soon after graduation, Scott joined a group of a few young farmers that decided to go tour one of the closest certified organic farms around, which was two hours away. He was impressed and amazed at how well they were doing. The "seed" was watered, but he was still convinced that it would not work on his soil type back home.

One of those neighbor boys, Jim Gasser, finally convinced his dad to let him give it a try. His dad gave him a small field not visible from the road. That young man became the first local, certified organic farmer in our neighborhood. His farm happened to be just across the road from ours. He proved to Scott that it could honestly be done—even in our area. The "seed" grew.

It was at this time that the law began to require farmers to go to classes to get a license in order to apply the modern chemicals. Scott wasn't interested in doing that, so he decided to hire it done. Something went wrong that year, and the early corn was severely stunted by the custom-applied herbicide. The only corn that grew well was where the sprayer missed.

Seizing the opportunity, Jim convinced Scott to try planting his remaining field using organic methods. He offered to do the weed control just to show Scott that it could be done—right on his own farm. It was some of his nicest corn that year. That was the last time Scott had chemicals sprayed on his crops.

Another aspect that encouraged me to investigate and then embrace organics was for the sake of Scott's health. He was coping so well with the here and now, but I remember him saying, "What about when I get old? It looks like things can be difficult with all your limbs. What if a stroke takes my whole left side?"

We know that according to Matthew 6:34 we should *take therefore no thought for the morrow: for the morrow shall take thought for the things of itself. Sufficient unto the day is the evil thereof.* Yet we are responsible for the choices we make, and we will deal with the consequences of those choices. I don't pretend to have all the answers, but I felt compelled to embrace organics so that I could do everything in my power to optimize his health.

Although the antibiotics that Scott got after his accident probably saved his life, we observed significant consequences in his health. Digging deeper we learned more and more about the medicines and their side effects. There is a time and a place for them. They do save lives, but we became very cautious in our administration of them either in the barn to the animals or in the house to the kids.

One of the hardest antibiotics for Scott to relinquish was dry-treat which is administering antibiotics to every cow about to dry off, even though she is perfectly healthy. That was confusing to me. When I innocently asked why he used routine antibiotics, it didn't go over very well. It was hard for Scott to have these methods questioned when he considered them tried and true.

It wasn't long after Scott's accident that we began to seriously consider transitioning the entire farm to organic. At that time, not only was there no market, but approved soil amendments, organic veterinary treatments, and beneficial resources were not yet readily available. We decided to go ahead and certify.

The next year there was still no market for organic milk. After scouring over the intimidating volume of certification paperwork, Scott finally threw them away. He concluded that he was going to farm organically but not certify.

Once again, Jim intervened and convinced Scott to try it for one more year. He felt there was going to be a market for organic milk very soon, and he wanted us to be ready. So we called the agency and ordered another set of forms.

Jim was right. We joined the Organic Valley Cooperative in 2003, and our first organic milk went out the lane in December. That is one decision we have never regretted.

So twenty years after the accident, we both find ourselves forty-something, with five sons and three daughters, four in-laws and six grandchildren. We have put the farm in a Limited Liability Corporation and brought the oldest three boys in as partners. All of the regular farm work is done by family members.

After cows being milked twice a day for over a hundred years by someone in our family, we hung up the milkers in the old barn for the last time on the morning of April 3, 2015. That evening we coaxed, pleaded, begged, chased, and downright pushed 160 cows through our new double-sixteen, parabone milking parlor built just east of the red bank barn. The old people and the old cows were the hardest to persuade that this was truly an improvement. Everybody told us it would take a few weeks before things would smooth out. Lo and behold! They did. As time passed we all seemed to adjust and genuinely enjoy the new setup.

We grow most of our own feed for the cows and food for the family. Scott and the boys have learned to process our own meat. We have also been producing our own maple syrup for about ten years. I cringe to use the saying "Many hands make light work" because of Scott's loss, but it still holds true today.

Chapter Thirteen

Do You Have Any Handicaps?

THE FIRST TIME SCOTT went to the License Bureau after his accident to renew his license, the clerk behind the counter asked, "Do you have any handicaps?"

Scott's simple answer was, "No."

Maybe she thought he was hard of hearing because she repeated the question—this time a little louder, "Do you have any handicaps?"

His answer was consistently, "No." So his license reflects that there are no handicaps. His only restriction is the same one that has been there since he was sixteen. He needs to wear corrective lenses when he drives.

Scott would occasionally drive our fifteen-passenger van for field trips for Heritage Private School, which invited our kids to come along. One particular trip was to the Federal Reserve in Cleveland. He had let the students and chaperons off by the door and went to find a parking space.

He had parked and put his quarters into the meter without a thought that all the meters on that street were blue. A police officer drove up, lowered his passenger window, and asked, "Do you realize that this is a handicapped parking place? There is a $250 fine for parking illegally here." Scott had not noticed that it was a handicapped parking place, but with some quick thinking he nonchalantly leaned in and rested his elbows on the car door making his prosthesis extremely visible. The officer stammered around and apologized, but then thinking again he started to see it differently. They both laughed good-naturedly, and Scott found a different place to park—much farther from the door.

Scott was attending a Sustainable Agriculture & Food Systems Funders conference in Denver, CO. The topic of conversation turned to the need for diversification of committee members. The group was admonished to make a concerted effort to include handicapped people, women, and minority races. Scott let them know in no uncertain terms that if he was selected to be on the committee because of the loss of his hand, he was not interested in continuing. He enjoys serving on committees *in spite* of his injury, but it is offensive if it is *because* of it.

He didn't want any special treatment. As he explained, "I don't think we should put a handicapped person, a woman, or a person of color on this committee just to fill a quota. I would gladly choose these people because of their abilities. The person should be chosen for their qualifications, not their circumstances." Scott felt that by setting these requirements, it was making him more aware of their cultural and physical differences rather than just seeing them as the way God made them—all equal in His eyes.

In 2003, when I was seven months pregnant with our sixth baby, a professor from Ohio State University invited Scott to take part in a marketing venture to Japan. It was to be an expense-paid trip with a man who had lived over there for years and claimed that he spoke better Japanese than English. (You surely couldn't prove it by me.) He was trying to open up a venue to sell the Japanese chemical-free soybeans from America to make tofu. The Japanese are very interested in not just their food, but how it was grown and the farmer who grew it. In the stores, they often post the farmer's picture right above the produce. Professor Moore knew why he wanted to bring American farmers with him. He had an agenda.

This would mean that Scott would be gone for six days, and the boys and I would take his place doing the chores. The baby was due in seven weeks. Under the circumstances, Scott didn't feel like there was any way he could go. "You have to!" I told him. "It's the chance of a lifetime!" I knew that Scott would delight in an opportunity like that to experience Japanese culture in the raw and meet new people. I couldn't stand to see him pass up this chance. I dropped to my knees right there on the kitchen floor and begged God to give us direction.

I persuaded Scott that we would be fine at home, and he boarded the plane—passport in hand—for a twelve-hour flight to the archipelago of Japan surrounded by the Pacific Ocean, the Sea of Okhotsk, East China Sea, Sea of Japan, and the Korea Strait. Now what would you expect a country surrounded by that much water to eat? Scott ate sushi, eel, octopus, clams, and about anything else that could live in or crawl out of the ocean. Almost everything was wrapped in a thin layer of kelp (aka seaweed). One of the group was craving something more similar to the American diet and ordered scrambled eggs for breakfast, but (alas!) even the eggs were mixed with fish and seasoned with seaweed. Only the orange juice and Pepsi were untainted!

There were two other farmers, Art and Perry, with Professor Moore and Scott. Once when they were together in their hotel room, Scott produced a bag of pretzels that I had sent along with him. You wouldn't think that a bag of pretzels that were all broken up from a long, international flight would have been a great treasure to those grown men, but they all—even Professor Moore—hungrily devoured the familiar taste of pretzels.

As their party stiffly sat Indian style at a table eighteen inches from the floor, the sea animals were still alive when they were brought out to them (and some of them seemingly still alive when they ate them). The chef would proceed to demonstrate how to "cook" them over a tiny candle while the clams would open and close as the heat reached them. If that isn't enough to make your stomach lurch! Scott thought they needed at least a half dozen more candles at the same time to get the job done. It's a good thing all they had to eat it with was chopsticks because that was as fast as they could chew and swallow their rubbery fare. It's also a good thing that Professor Moore took the farmer and not the farmer's wife. I'll stick to beef and chicken!

The Japanese were not big on desserts. Scott brought home a sample of some of their delicacies. What I remember most was the orange peels dipped in dark chocolate. I thought it was actually kind of good, but then I do have an affinity for dark chocolate. None of the rest of my family agreed with me. I can tell you one thing for sure, I'd rather eat that than some eel half-cooked over a tiny, make-believe bonfire!

Another discovery Scott made was that their beverage of choice is *saké*. Now *saké* is a fermented rice wine with a higher alcohol content than wine or beer. Scott remembered well his surgeon's stern warning, and he had to do some quick thinking.

Japan is a country steeped in culture and traditions. It was very important in what order of rank they sat down to the table. It was even important in what order they walked down the street if their Japanese colleagues were looking out the window. About three blocks away from their business meeting at the tofu factory with their soybeans in tow, Professor Moore told them, "Now don't walk down the street like a bunch of Americans." He believed that his last prospective deal was lost because they sat in the wrong order at the table. He drilled them very thoroughly that they should follow the culture completely.

This created a problem for Scott because it was considered very rude if he didn't eat and drink all of what was served to him. To have left an unfinished drink would have been offensive. He struck a deal with one of the other farmers. When Perry finished his *saké*, he swapped his empty goblet for Scott's full one. Scott then drank Pepsi, which was his only other choice.

Japan is a very clean and tidy country. Scott remembered once when there was a piece of trash on the sidewalk that looked so out-of-place that he and Art both stooped to pick it up at once. They never wore their street shoes in a building. In a store, they would take off their shoes, line them up at the door, and shop in their socks. In the hotel, there were sandals (like our flip-flops) provided by each doorway that they were expected to slip on after they took their shoes off. Scott remembered, "We were walking off the back of the sandals because all of them were too small." They could wear their street clothes to their rooms, but then they were expected to put on "this thing that wrapped around us" called a kimono.

Restrooms were another adventure. Most of the toilets were level with the floor. For some reason, toilet paper was not provided in the restrooms. He had to collect Kleenexes whenever he could find them. Some stores would pass out little tissue packs as advertisement. He was soon to realize how valuable they were. If he happened to be lucky enough to find an American-style commode, it was by trial-and-error that he figured out what the buttons meant. He was never sure if he was going to hear birds chirping or feel a spray of water.

Professor Moore didn't stick to Tokyo; he took them into the heart of Japan. Real Japan. Out where they were, Professor Moore said most of the locals had never seen Americans. If the Americans got into an elevator, the Japanese would promptly get out even if it wasn't their destination. When they stepped off the train, the Japanese would jump on their bicycles and flee. They were shocked to see Caucasian men come to their restaurants and hotels. These Americans were giants compared to their small statures.

At the hotels, the tiny female attendants clip-clopping in very high-heeled shoes insisted on carrying the Americans' luggage. Now each of them had two suitcases, one with their clothes and one with over sixty pounds of chemical-free soybeans from

America. The farmers looked on in disbelief. Professor Moore shrugged and told them, "Let them do it. It's their culture."

When the little women welcomed them to the hotel with a string of words that were totally unintelligible to the farmers, Scott grinned at Art and told him, "I think she said she wants your luggage." Always ready for fun, Art retorted, "I think she said, 'Go jump in a lake!'" The two of them ducked around the corner and doubled over with laughter.

Once when Scott was following a Japanese man through a doorway, the man glanced back and deliberately let the door slam in his face. The embarrassed interpreter of their group apologized, "I'm sorry! We in Japan aren't very kind to the handicapped!"

"That's okay," Scott assured her. "I'm not handicapped."

Scott returned home to a very warm welcome. I hadn't known that six days could seem so long. I will confess to a few times of serious doubting. "Why, oh why, did I ever tell him that he should go?!" But when he was home safe and sound, we were both glad he had gotten the chance.

A few weeks after he had returned home, Clark Steven was born on Father's Day, on that beautiful spring morning. He was our first child born at home. The other children were at church with their grandparents. They drew numbers on the way home to see what order they would get to hold their new baby brother.

Scott once read a quote in the *Reader's Digest* by Jim Stovall that he found very inspiring: "I've seen people recover physical abilities, yet never get over emotional trauma after a serious accident. I've seen other people overcome the psychological and emotional trauma of a serious illness even though they may never fully regain their physical capabilities. Which is the greater healing? Which is the better recovery? If I had the option of choosing between a mediocre life with eyesight or the life I have today, *even though I am blind,* I'd stay blind and keep the life I have."

There it is again. It's a choice. The person who can but won't has the greater handicap.

Chapter Fourteen

What Did You Learn?

Soon after the accident, Scott's uncle asked him what he learned while he was in the baler. Scott thought a moment and replied, "My right arm was in excruciating pain, the belts were smoking from friction and I could have burned to death at any minute, my clothes were ripped off and fed into the rolls making the rest of me freezing cold, I could have bled to death, the baler was lurching and making horrible sounds, the smell of burning coats, rubber, flesh, and bone was nauseating, but my God was big enough to grant me a complete peace." My God was big enough...

As we often find in life, we don't appreciate what we have until it is gone. Many times I have gazed at his remaining left hand and admired its strength and ruggedness. I'm reminded of one of my mom's favorite songs:

"Waste not, want not, is a lesson I would teach,
Let this be your motto, Son, and practice what you preach,
Never let your chances like a sunbeam pass you by,
You'll never miss the water till the well runs dry."*

We have occasionally been asked to speak to groups about Scott's accident. Sometimes Scott says, "I just don't feel like climbing back into that machine." He usually does it anyway. In preparation for a presentation Scott came up with a list he called, "Ten Things I've Learned in the Baler." Incidentally, it turned out to be twelve things.

1. Quality time is a poor excuse for quantity time. Some people like to take a lavish vacation as an excuse for not just being with their families in normal life.

2. Children grow up—with or without us. Cherish the moments as they come.

3. "Standard of Living" and "Quality of Life" are not the same thing. Christ said in Luke 12:15, *A man's life consisteth not in the abundance of the things which he possesseth.*

4. Obey God regardless of the cost. When you are facing death, it becomes very clear that God's Word is final. We will be judged by what the Bible says—not by what we think it says.

5. No matter where you are…there you are. Every day many people load up their moving vans and go from here to there; the same day others go from there to here. They both think they are moving to a better place to live, but they take themselves with them. Make sure that you aren't the reason you don't like where you are.

6. Don't ever say, "If I could only lie in bed until I was tired of it." Scott used to say that before the accident happened. Sometimes he just got tired of getting up at 3:30AM. It didn't take him very long to realize that the ability to get out of bed is a wonderful privilege—even very early in the morning to milk cows.

7. It's not what happens *to* you but what happens *in* you that matters.

*"You'll Never Miss the Water 'Till the Well Runs Dry" by Roland Howard

8. You *can* make a difference. There was a little village beside the sea whose whole livelihood came from harvesting clams. There was a bad storm that washed thousands of them up on the shore, and the villagers were devastated. There was a little boy who was walking along, picking them up one by one, and throwing them back into the water. An old man reprimanded him that his actions were futile and said, "There are so many here, Son. You just can't make a difference." The little boy picked up another one, tossed it back into the sea, and replied, "I made a difference for that one!"

9. There is some earthly value to Lamaze class. Using the breathing techniques and the screwdriver as a focal point while in the bone-grinding embrace of the baler, Scott was able to maintain consciousness, which may have saved his life.

10. A man with experience is never at the mercy of a man with an argument. This is one of Scott's favorite sayings when someone comes at him with some haughty, long-winded dissertation that they don't really know anything about. The social media platform does nothing to make the information true or the speaker an expert. His boys will tell you that he's very open to new ideas. He often lets them try new things that he does not think will work, but change just for the sake of change is not all that great.

11. A list of "Ten Things I've Learned" left in your back pocket is no match for the Maytag.

12. It takes a man to cry.

When we are asked to speak publicly, Scott usually delivers a specific message to the young people in the audience. His purpose is to convey the importance of understanding consequences for disobedience:

"My dad told me many times as a young boy never to get off the tractor with the machine running, and I told him I wouldn't. I disobeyed my dad that day. I knew better. I lost my right hand. My dad forgave me, my God forgave me, and after many years I forgave myself, but I didn't get my hand back. There's a price. We can be forgiven. It's not held against us in eternity, but there's a price to pay and to carry for sin."

Another point that Scott believes is important to make to an audience is to nurture the relationships that we share—especially with those who are closest to us. In his words, "When I went out that day, I had *no* thought of not coming back in. Make sure you are satisfied with how you left your relationships in case you can't come back. Make sure they know that you love them."

One of Scott's uncles who had been through a difficult bout with cancer posed a question to him, "Would you give it all back if you could have your hand back?" Scott's reply was, "No. I'd have to say no, but I'd take a horrible beating to not have to go through it all again."

I've heard it said that most of what we see still depends on what we are looking for. I have noticed a specific difference in myself based on the thoughts I choose to dwell on. Clark innocently told me, "Sometimes the day can look so dreary, but I can change that by cleaning my glasses." He said that as he was wiping his lenses, but I thought it was profound. The eye has been referred to as the window of the soul, and sometimes we might need to "clean our glasses."

After one presentation during a question and answer period, someone asked, "Smooth sailing does not make good sailors, so what did you learn during that time?"

Scott gave him the same response that he gave his uncle 19 years earlier. His God was big enough to give him complete peace even though he was facing death and in excruciating pain. Then he added, "We don't know what's ahead of us as Christians, but if we are called upon to die for Him, He is able to provide the grace and strength in that hour—and not a minute before. It won't be there. We don't have it now. It doesn't make sense. But in the moment, it's there." God's grace is for what is, not what if. He is able...

Then the question was posed to me, "What about you, Charlene?"

I was unprepared for that and stammered something about needing more time to think about it. Later, I sent him this letter:

When Scott and I spoke in Sunday School about the accident, you made a comment that smooth sailing does not make good sailors. You followed that statement with, "So what did you learn during the hard times?" My initial response was something like, "I need a few months to think about that. The thing that baffles me the most is that my joy is fuller and my peace is deeper when (or maybe because) I am hurting so badly."

For some reason, your question has lingered with me, "What *do* I learn in the hard times?" I awoke this morning with that question preoccupying my mind. It would be nice if I could say that because of the hard times I am unendingly patient, ever humble, never angry, not bound by earthly thoughts and endeavors or "cares of this life," without selfish motives or ill intentions, and never speak an unkind word. Some days I marvel that He does not give up on me. It reminds me of a song, "He must have lovin' eyes to take a good look at me and not even criticize."* The closer I walk beside Him, the more I long to be like Him and to please Him.

Maybe what I learned is not so much about me, but what I learned about God through the tough times. The nearer I come to Him, the more aware I am of my own imperfections within. His presence contrasts with who I am if I am honest with myself. Yet, overshadowing that feeling of unworthiness that His nearness creates in me is the abounding love I feel *from* and *for* Him—in spite of who I am. It reflects back to His sacrifice at the cross that covers my sin and makes me able to be His child.

I once told Scott when my heart was throbbing in pain that I crawled up on God's lap, laid my head on His shoulder, and wept. He (Scott) replied that he was on the other knee. Another time, I confided to a friend that in my dark night I felt like God had

* "He Must Have Lovin' Eyes" by Phil Johnson

wrapped His arms around me. She told me, "I specifically prayed for you that God would wrap His arms around you." I was in awe. I don't think I will ever forget that. Often when someone is on my heart and in my prayers and I don't even know what to ask for them, I ask God to wrap His arms around them. Because that friend's prayers were answered, it gives me courage and faith to pray the same for someone else. I crave His presence more than His gifts. I have even felt that I am addicted to His presence…to the point that it turns the hard times into hidden blessings.

"Thank you for the valley I walked through today.
The darker the valley the more I learned to pray.
I found you where the lily is blooming by the way.
So I thank you for the valley I walked through today.

Life can't be all sunshine or the flowers would die;
The rivers would be desert, all barren and dry.
Life can't be all blessing or there'd be no need to pray,
So I thank you for the valley I walked through today.

Thank you for every hill I climbed,
For every time the sun didn't shine.
Thank you for every lonely night
I prayed till I knew everything was alright
And I thank you for the valley I walked through today."*

Because God's love became so real and near to me when I needed it so desperately, it became more natural to in turn love other people—even people who are not just like me, in spite of their faults or mistakes just as I have faults and make mistakes. I cannot manufacture love. I can only abide in the Vine (John 15), and He pours His love through me to others. In loving more, we judge less. Having said that, we still cling to the Bible knowing that we will be judged by what it says not by what we think it

*"Thank You for the Valley" by Dottie Rambo

102

says or wish it said. Love without truth is hypocrisy and deception. Truth without love is brutality. We need to be "speaking the truth in love" (Eph. 4:15). I wish my love could be even purer and deeper. I wish it was easier to forgive those who cause pain.

Another thing that hard times taught me was to trust Him. Trust is a word that has many different levels. I don't know how deep it can go, but I know I have been taught to leave things to His care that I wanted to try to take care of myself. By nature, I am a fixer and a fighter. I want to fix the problem and fight for what I believe is right. He has taught me to leave it with Him… and rest in that. When we want to seek our own vengeance, He reminds us that vengeance is His. When we want to come to our own defense, He reminds us that He is our Defender (Isaiah 41, 48, and 66; Psalm 18; Genesis 15).

Another favorite song (I have a lot of those):

"If on a quiet sea
Toward heaven we calmly sail
With grateful hearts, O God, to Thee
We'll own the favoring gale.

But should the surges rise
And rest delay to come
Blest be the tempest, kind the storm
That drives us nearer Home.*

In other words, we will be grateful for smooth sailing, but when He sees fit to allow the tempest, we will bless the storm that drives us to the arms of God."

*"If on a Quiet Sea" by Agustus M Toplady

CHAPTER FIFTEEN

From the Heart

AS I WAS FINISHING up this book, I became aware that it was not quite complete without the perspectives and viewpoints of others who were close to us. I asked them to share…from the heart.

I found Dave, Scott's oldest brother, in his milking parlor one morning with my notepad in hand. He is a man of few words, and I thought that I'd get more information out of him if I talked to him in his natural habitat. At one point, he covered his face with his hands and choked back a sob. This was Dave's story:

We had cut a bunch of firewood all summer long to use in our wood-burning stove in order to save on our heating bill. I had just got the liquefied petroleum gas bill and was disgusted at how high it was when I was trying so hard to keep it low. When I heard about Scott, I realized that I had been in a warm house that day while my brother was out in the freezing cold. It put it all back into perspective.

I did Dad's chores that morning for him because he needed to take Mom to have some testing done at the hospital. Then because Jan had not been feeling well lately, I told her to make a doctor's appointment, and I would stay with the kids. I planned to go in to work later when she got back home.

When I got the call from Sterling Farm Equipment that Scott needed me so badly, I wondered, "What am I going to do with my kids?" I turned around to see the garage door going up. Jan was home.

When I got to the accident, Dale Glessner, Sterling's EMT, was trying the Jaws of Life, but it wasn't going so well for him. He told me, "I'll try one more time. We just got this thing, and I want to try it out." However, because the rolls were round, metal objects, as the tension increased, it shot the Jaws out.

I asked Scott where his torches were. He answered, "There's one in the machine shed and one in the barn. The oxygen tank in the machine shed is about empty. You have to get the torch in the barn or switch the tanks." Mike Guidetti went to get them.

"Don't let the sparks get on him," I advised. They found a piece of cardboard from the machine shed to shield Scott from the torch's spatter of sparks.

I cut down through the metal pieces until I was almost done. "I'm just about through," I warned the EMTs. "I don't know what's going to happen. Be ready to catch him." I finished the cut and spread the rolls apart. He dropped like a rag into their arms.

"His arm!" I groaned. I don't remember a lot about the rest of that day.

One of my aunts called on the phone. I told them he would probably lose his hand. Trying to be optimistic, she challenged, "You don't really know though." I just told her, "You didn't see him in the baler."

Later people would ask me how I did it. I don't really know

how I did it. You don't think about that at the time. He was stuck; I had to get him out. He was cold, but he was still alive. I didn't realize then that it was so serious.

I still do dumb things. Then I think, "Why did you do that? Your brother lost his hand doing things like that."

Scott's mom has always been the epitome of a godly woman. I cherish her friendship and treasure the expressions of her memories. These are her words: It was so cold outside. When Everett and I walked into the house, the warmth of the kitchen felt so good. I immediately heard the telephone answering machine beeping incessantly. There were several messages; they were all about Scott. He was in serious trouble, with his arm caught in the round baler.

We immediately headed out the door and up to the farm where I grew up. We wove our way through vehicles and people to find Scott. After all, he was our son. We caught a glimpse of him on the stretcher as they were stabilizing him before departure. I was so glad to get to talk to him briefly before he left.

I turned around to see Lilas, Charlene's mom, crying. She's a tough lady, and I had never seen her cry before. We were all numb with disbelief. This couldn't be happening.

Since Lilas had their children, there was only one choice for us. We were going wherever they were taking Scott. It was at Wadsworth-Rittman that we were delighted to hear the first good news—his elbow was not damaged. We were soon en route to St. Thomas Hospital. We didn't know the way and neither of us liked city driving, so we followed my brother-in-law.

Then the heavy time of waiting began. We had lots of family there to comfort and pray with us; it almost seemed like we filled up the waiting room. I can still see the surgeon finally coming to give us a report. He was kind and considerate and tried to be encouraging…but he had to amputate Scott's right hand. Everett and I were devastated, but we still had Scott. That was a lot to be thankful for. We could think of little else.

We came home and somehow got through that first night. Early the next morning, Everett went downstairs to the washroom to dress in his farm clothes for the morning milking. I heard this heart-wrenching, mournful weeping. It was a father crying for his son. He said, "If only this could have been me instead of Scott."

Memories of Scott's carefree, happy childhood and teen years flooded me and played its scenes over and over in my mind. I had been so thankful that he and his family were getting established on the farm where I grew up. My youngest brother, George, needed help which presented an opportunity for Scott. We had one farm and four boys.

Farming consists of long hours and hard work. Would this change Scott's chance to buy my dad's farm? Would he still be able to do the necessary work and support his family? How would he handle this devastating loss? How would Charlene and their children handle this turn of events?

Parents often keenly feel like they are going through things right with their children. When things go well, we rejoice with them. When the children suffer, we suffer right with them. Everett and I went to the hospital as much as we could and were there with Charlene during surgeries.

Mothers, by nature, want to fix all the hurts and make everything better. I felt totally out of control. I could do nothing. We had to watch helplessly while our son and his family went through so much. Our family, our large extended families, our church, and our friends were so kind and wonderful. We called often on our heavenly Father. He carried us through.

I don't see how anyone could have handled this better than Charlene. She was simply amazing. She often spoke kindly of Scott. Mothers really appreciate that. Without her help and support this accident would have a much different outcome. The Lord has certainly blessed them in every way.

A few years ago our Sunday School teacher invited Scott to come to our class and tell us how this accident has changed his life. He mentioned that he feels so badly that he is not the man Charlene married. I thought to myself, "No, he isn't the same man; he is an even better man."

Scott's brother, Steve, was the next one older than him; they did a lot together growing up. He was working on his boss's cabin as the foreman of his crew when his wife, Mary Lynn, called, "Scott's caught in a baler. They can't get him out. Your dad wants you here because he's so shook up." Steve and his whole crew left the job right then and there.

That night following the accident, Steve turned and rolled in his bed for a long time unable to drop off to sleep. Finally, he looked at the clock and did a quick mental calculation: three hours! That was a long time, and Scott was caught in the baler that long! That didn't help sleep come any quicker.

One of their cousins came to see Scott in the hospital and said (pun intended), "Let me know if I can ever lend you a hand." Steve said, "To this day, when someone offers to lend me a hand, my mind still goes to that."

For the first year or so all Steve could see was Scott's injury. This was his little brother he grew up with and wrestled with. It hurt for a long time.

He evidently eventually got over some of his sympathy. One day about ten years later, Steve saw the hammock that I had gotten Scott for Father's Day swinging empty in the breeze. He mentioned, "It's a good thing Scott wasn't lying in that thing or I would have had to dump him out."

Growing up, Steve was the only left-handed one in the family. After the accident, Scott remarked, "Two of us are left-handed and two of us are right-handed." Steve momentarily forgot, "No. I'm the only left-handed one."

Steve said, "This has affected everybody downstream and upstream. I don't think Dad ever really got over it."

Doyle turned six during Scott's stay at Akron General. Doyle told me, "I don't remember very much from that time. Grandma picked me up at school in her gray station wagon and explained that Daddy had an accident and went to the hospital. They took us up to see him, and I hid behind the recliner in the hospital room and sobbed.

"When he got VRE, it was very disconcerting. Grandma was making a lot of phone calls. Even though I couldn't understand what was happening, I knew something was *terribly* wrong.

"On the day he got his prosthesis, we ran out to the van to meet him as soon as he got home. We wanted to see this thing! I asked him how much it could hold. He told me to grab on, and he picked me up with it and carried me a short distance.

"From my perspective, it's almost frustrating trying to answer questions about my memories from that time. It is such a part of normalcy that it seems odd to write a book about it."

I sensed those very same sentiments from Doyle's siblings. They love their dad fiercely just like he is.

RoseMary said, "He seems just like any other dad. I don't even think I knew he was missing his hand for a long time." Doyle's four-year-old son, Josiah, recently asked her in a confused, surprised tone, "Is his-um-is his arm all gone?"

Doyle ended our brief interview with, "One thing that really makes me mad is when someone babies him. At the same time, if there's something we boys can do to prevent tendonitis or carpal tunnel, we are quick to do it!"

Toby overheard Doyle's comment. As an ever-loyal and maybe even biased son, Toby completely agreed, adding, "Yeah! When people baby him, and he could do a better job than they could!"

Melody explained, "Some people think it makes me nervous to talk about it...but it doesn't.

"When I look for Dad, I look for his face not his hand.

"I have always liked Dad's hook because it is the perfect grip for my hand.

"One time I had a Band-Aid on my thumb, so I asked Mom to button my shirt. She told me that Daddy does it with one hand all the time. When I thought about it, I was amazed at all that he does with one hand."

Nelson commented, "They say that we view our heavenly Father the way we view our earthly father. I didn't give it a lot of thought until I realized that I unintentionally think of God with one hand—one big hand." Warren agreed, "I definitely think of God with one hand."

"As a boy, the hook symbolized manliness to me," Nelson added.

Toby said, "I used to think it was odd that Dad's friends didn't have a hook."

Clark told me, "All those years I saw those strips on his legs (scars from the skin grafting), I thought it was from his long johns." That one brought the house down!

Lynelle was 4 years, one week, and one day old when the accident happened, and her memories are delicate, but as she dug them out and dusted them off, there were more there than she had first realized. She discovered sensitive emotions appeared to be mixed in with those memories as well. They were boxed up and shelved together. She shared what she found:

Nelson (1½ years old) and I were in the van alone; Mom had left. The van was running, and her window was down. It felt like a long time. Sensing that something was very wrong but not knowing what it was, I was scared that the van was going to blow up. Fear and insecurity smothered me, and I started crying. Soon Nelson joined me. Dad was just a few feet away, so I asked him to turn the van off.

With a strange look on his face, he said, "I can't, Nellie. I'm stuck." That didn't make sense either because Dad could always fix my little-girl problems. More fear. More insecurity. More tears.

The next thing I remember is watching out the big picture window with Grandma Rufener as the ambulance took my daddy out the lane to who-knows-where for who-knows-what.

My two brothers and I stayed at Grandma's house. She helped us cut out big paper hearts at the kitchen table to take to Daddy at the hospital. Doyle (almost six years old) had a loud prayer at the supper table asking God to make our daddy get better.

Then we got to go see him. My eyes swept over the strange, unfamiliar room until I saw the daddy I loved. I felt so tangled up inside. I wanted to be close to him, but fear and shyness churned in my head and intimidated me. He looked so different lying in the bed covered with all those white sheets.

We enjoyed our time at Grandma's, but I was so glad when Daddy got to come home. As long as I had him, I didn't care whether he had one hand or two.

When he first got his prosthesis, we kids went running out to meet him in the driveway. What a fascinating—and maybe a little intimidating—contraption that was to us. He invited us to put our finger in his hook, and he'd lightly grasp it. It was a warm-up method on his part to show us that we didn't need to be afraid of it. It worked. He often shows it to other children when he sees that they've noticed it.

I was excited that he also had an attachment that really looked like his hand, and at first I wanted him to wear it…until he tried it on. It looked so real, but when you touched it, it was cold and hard and stiff. When he moved the fingers, it creaked eerily like rubber. I just didn't feel like I was holding Daddy's hand. His hook was better. It wasn't Daddy either, but it wasn't pretending to be.

We soon adjusted to this new normal. I don't ever remember being embarrassed that he only had one hand. If anything, I respected him more. We didn't realize how different he probably felt or the phantom pain he carried. As we got older, bits and pieces came together that began to show us how much he was really dealing with.

He never complained about his pain. On the days when it hurt the worst, he generally got quieter and would get a faraway look in his eyes like he was thinking. He could have made our lives miserable, but he chose not to with God's help. We never saw Dad having a pity party for himself.

One year we got a foosball table for Christmas. It got a lot of use for a while. "Practice makes improved," and our skills sharpened. Somehow, though, it seemed like Dad was always a little better than we were. He finally informed us with a big grin that we were using too many hands! I think we actually tried using only one hand, but that didn't seem to help us beat him either.

There weren't many things we got to help Dad do as a result of his injury. He just didn't need it. He'd lace his work shoes a special way and tie his hood strings (and ours) with his teeth and one hand. If he did come across something, he'd cheerfully let us help. The only reason I didn't want to button his long sleeve shirt cuff was because I knew he wished he could do it himself.

We tried to remember to turn the vehicle steering wheel to a spot where he could reach the ignition through the steering wheel easier before we turned off the engine. I don't think I've ever seen a car with the ignition on the left side. (When Jessica heard this, the lightbulb went on. She exclaimed, "So that's why Nelson always turned the steering wheel after the car was in park!")

I enjoyed going to farmers' meetings with him. When I sat beside him, I'd get to provide the second hand to clap with when the speaker sat down. I soon found out—good, bad, or otherwise—that most people knew who the "one-armed man" was. If someone asked my name, I'd say, "Lynelle Stoller." That might merit a polite smile or nod. When I added, "I'm Scott's daughter," the light would usually go on; if not, I might add, "He lost his hand in a farming accident." Then most people would know right where I belonged.

For Dad, it was probably a little more inconvenient. They'd say, "Hi, Scott!" He would give a friendly hello, and they'd visit like old friends for a little while before they moved on. "Hey, Dad, who was that?" I'd ask. Dad would say, "I don't have a clue. He knew who I was, so I felt funny asking his name!"

When I was five, I thought ten was big. When I was ten, I thought fifteen was big. Throughout my childhood, I thought Dad and Mom were "big" when the accident happened. Then when my husband, Craig, and I were expecting our third child, it dawned on me how close we were to the stage of life Dad and Mom were when he lost his arm.

Suddenly, I found myself trying on "Mom's shoes" when Craig suffered a TBI (Traumatic Brain Injury) from a fall as the result of a farming accident. Mom was human. Just like me. She wasn't big. Not at all. She loved her husband. So much. And she wanted him back. So badly. But she wanted to be willing to accept God's will, and she wanted Him to use it to His glory. Thankfully, Craig experienced an exceptional recovery.

In all their affliction he was afflicted, and the angel of his presence saved them: in his love and in his pity he redeemed them; and he bare them, and carried them all the days of old (Isaiah 63:9).

Just a note: I was very interested to hear what Doyle and Lynelle would have to say about their dad's accident. They were our only children who were old enough to remember. One thing that became so clear to me is that if a family experiences trauma, it is *so* important that they explain to the small children in simple terms what is happening. Children are very quick to feel the tension that "something is wrong." As adults, we tend to talk over their heads as though they don't understand. The children often lack the confidence to ask the questions burning in their hearts. Keep the explanations age appropriate. If they ask what time it is, don't tell them how a clock works.

Naomi met our family as a teenager. She said, "I am so blessed and privileged to be a part of the Scott & Charlene Stoller family. I first met them in 2007 when I was fifteen. Four years later I married their oldest son. My dream of being a farmer's wife came true.

"I hardly ever think of it that my father-in-law is missing a hand. One day I observed Doyle biting his fingernails. I said, 'I bet even your dad doesn't bite his fingernails. I bet he uses a nail clipper.' Doyle gave me a funny look, and it was then I realized what I had said.

"Scott is amazing. He can do anything—going up and down silos, climbing up ladders to paint rooftops, milking cows, driving tractors, etc. His determined attitude is an inspiration to me. He doesn't just sit there and feel sorry for himself.

"He is a very good grandpa to our children. Sometimes when they are walking together, Josiah will reach up and hold onto his hook.

"I'm so proud of you, Dad!"

Jessica, on the other hand, knew our family all of her life. She expressed herself, "I have always (even as a young girl who didn't know him well at all) respected him very highly. He used to drive on our field trips, and I loved having him come. He was ALWAYS happy!

"I have always been intrigued with his arm: what muscles came from where, how the phantom pain works, etc. I remember asking him to show me under the sock one time when we were engaged. It wasn't because I looked down on it; I actually thought more highly of him because of it. I don't know what he was like with two hands, but without knowing that, I still like the Scott with one hand better!

"I honestly feel VERY honored to have joined such an incredible family! I couldn't have asked for a better husband, mother/ father-in-law, and siblings. You are so wonderful to me and I hope I can be the same back to you."

Dale Hess had picked up the milk at both Scott's home farm and his grandparents' farm. He had watched Scott grow from a little boy to an adult; he saw him make the transition from his parents' farm to his grandparents' farm. About two days after the accident occurred, Dale came to the farm to pick up the milk. He believed in Scott. His words weren't flowery, but he told Uncle George, "You see…he'll get it!"

Uncle George said, "I thought there would be quite a few times he'd need help, but it didn't happen much. I suppose if it was all added up, there were more times I asked him for help."

Aaron Arnold was Scott's Agricultural Education Instructor and FFA Adviser. He summed it up like this: I can honestly say that I do not remember where I was when I received word that Scott had been in an accident. But, I do recall thinking, "Oh no, not again!" You see, when Scott was in high school, he was "experimenting" with the oxy-acetylene torch at the home farm and nearly blinded himself from an explosion! I remember Scott telling me the doctors said that his contact lenses saved his sight. When I heard about the baler accident, the notes to his family scribbled on the baler, the weather conditions that saved his life, and the loss of an arm, I firmly believed that Someone had some big plans for this man.

I remember visiting Scott in the hospital with my wife, Katy, and three children, Ryan (8), Travis (6), and Marie (3). Scott told us he had visited other patients on his floor. It stuck in my mind how he described how fortunate he was and that he would never want to trade places with anyone else! I was so impressed that he moved around visiting others and still maintained a bright outlook on his situation. My children remember that visit to this day. As a matter of fact, it is one of my daughter's first memories.

As time passed and Scott and Charlene's scars healed, I would ask them to talk to the members in my FFA Chapter concerning safety and decision-making around equipment. Their message was always well received. The students were attentive and curious with questions. Charlene would always emphasize and illustrate how the accident doesn't just affect the victim, but also the impact it has on the entire family.

I have since retired from teaching Agricultural Education full-time and now teach part-time at Ohio State – Agricultural Technical Institute in Wooster, Ohio. I still ask Scott and Charlene to come and talk to my class – Equipment Operation and Maintenance. The students at the college level are just as attentive as those in the past. When I ask the students how they liked the speakers, a typical response is, "We need to hear more people like that." Scott and Charlene's message is definitely heard, loudly and clearly. They summarize it like this, "Life is not about what happens to you, but how you respond to what happens to you!"

Chapter Sixteen

Overcoming

OVERCOMING. NOT OVERCAME—that was yesterday. Not will overcome—that is tomorrow. Overcoming—that is today…right now. We each have obstacles in our lives. Overcoming is not something that is once-and-done. It takes a lifetime to accomplish. We can't do it alone. We need Jesus. Oh, we try for a while. We might even succeed for a while. But He loves us too much to let us go on and on thinking we are the self-sufficient master of our own destiny.

So when those trials come—whether heartaches, temptations, disappointments, disasters, death, traumas, or all of the above— we are faced with choices. They can be stumbling blocks or stepping stones. We can wallow in self-pity and all the poor-me-isms the devil provides us, or we can take a deep breath, embrace the struggle, and trust the Master for His strength and wisdom.

For Scott, these struggles include the awkwardness of looking "different," the stiff challenges of performing his tasks and duties with one hand when most of us use two hands, and coping with the constant pain as a result of the physical trauma of 1997. While not nearly as serious, it is also being only left-handed in what he calls "an amazingly right-handed world."

Having previously been right-handed, it is frustrating to him how most power tools, scissors, and control levers are geared towards the right hand. Even a towel dispenser that instructs, "Pull with both hands," is a reminder to him that it can't be done. On most days it is not an issue. Once in a while it feels like a jab in the ribs.

Scott has never been one to do a job halfway. One of his favorite teachers was Art Oswald who was the instructor for industrial arts. He was well-known for having students who regularly turned out projects that won "Best of Show" at both the county and state fairs. While working on his grandfather clock in high school, he remembers asking Mr. Oswald, "Is this good enough?" Mr. Oswald answered, "It's good enough for a red ribbon (second place)." Scott didn't want a red ribbon; he wanted a blue one. He decided to work a little harder at it…and his grandfather clock took "Best of Show" at the Ohio State Fair.

It still haunts him today when he's working on something and tells himself, "That's good enough." In his mind he hears Mr. Oswald say, "It's good enough for a red ribbon." Scott doesn't like to settle for less than his best effort. I believe that trait has spurred him on many times to tackle a project that would look insurmountable to some of the rest of us.

Scott was naturally born right-handed. The intriguing thing is that once his right hand was gone, his brain automatically made the left hand dominant. He said, "Before I came to from the amputation surgery, my left hand was coordinated." The left hand now feels so natural to him that it feels like his "right hand." In fact, right and left still confuse him to this day. So when he gives directions to "turn left" or "turn right," I wait for him to reassess his instruction. He's correct about fifty percent of the time.

He also gets confused about which way to tighten a bolt or a jar lid. He has to stop and think, "Righty—tighty. Lefty—loosey."

At first, his brain flip also caused his signature to be backwards. He had to concentrate to write from left to right. He wanted to write from right to left, and when he did that his signature was a perfect mirror image of his signature from before the accident.

Scott knew that I was very interested in pencil sketching, and we are fortunate enough to have a very talented art teacher who lives nearby and gives lessons. I didn't think I had time to take an art class, but Scott insisted. So I did, and I loved it. Now I say that when I grow up and become a famous artist someday, Scott wants my masterpiece to be a picture of the gates of heaven with a rubbish heap off to the side. It will include wheelchairs, crutches, canes, braces, slings, walker…and prosthetics. It's going to be titled, "Perfectly Whole—Body, Mind, and Soul."

January 16, 2017, marked 20 years since the accident. Twenty years! There are lots of things that come our way that we wouldn't choose, but knowing that they all pass through God's hand first and that He won't allow more than we can bear (I Corinthians 10:13) gives us confidence to go on. Scott has mentioned, "I think *He* thinks I'm stronger than I think I am."

As you know, Scott canceled the pityparty years ago and carries out his duties with incredible ability. The downside is that when some of the rest of us so much as smash a thumb or get a splinter we don't really feel like we should complain very much.

We can't hide from the reality of our situations. One morning you wake up normal; by nightfall you may feel anything but normal. We fight the thing that hurts us. How can this happen to me? Accidents happen to other people, but not to me! Not so.

There were many, many tears and heartaches that sunk deeper inside me than I even knew I went, but I can honestly say that through Scott's accident and aftermath, neither of us ever blamed God or were angry at Him. If He saw fit to allow this thing to come to pass in our lives, then it must be for our ultimate good.

The thing that always astounds me is that it seems like the gouges cut deep into my heart by pain and suffering made more room for the fullness of joy and peace that Jesus brings when we trust Him with our whole selves and every situation.

I cringe to bring up Romans 8:28, *All things work together for good to them that love God,* because it is used so often in the Christian world that I fear it becomes stale, but it is so real to me. When troubles come, I often think, "I wonder how He'll bring good out of THIS!" If we will dry our eyes, still our hearts, and trust the Master, He always comes through. It may not be in a tangible, earthly sense but rather in a spiritual sense. His nearness defies expression.

> One ship goes east, and another west
> By the selfsame winds that blow
> 'Tis the set of the sails and not the gales
> That determines the way they go.
> Like the winds of the sea are the ways of time
> As we journey along through life
> 'Tis the set of the soul that determines the goal
> And not the calm or the strife.
> -Ella Wheeler Wilcox

We must always remember to focus on what we have rather than what we have lost.